MARTIN LUTHER KING, JR.

MARTIN LUTHER KING, JR.

A Biography

Roger Bruns

GREENWOOD BIOGRAPHIES

GREENWOOD PRESS
WESTPORT, CONNECTICUT · LONDON

Library of Congress Cataloging-in-Publication Data

Bruns, Roger.
   Martin Luther King, Jr. : a biography / Roger Bruns.
      p. cm. — (Greenwood biographies, ISSN 1540–4900)
   Includes bibliographical references and index.
   ISBN 0–313–33686–5
   1. King, Martin Luther, Jr., 1929–1968. 2. African Americans—Biography.
3. Civil rights workers—United States—Biography. 4. Baptists—United States—
Clergy—Biography. 5. African Americans—Civil rights—History—20th century.
I. Title. II. Series.
E185.97.K5B77 2006
323.092—dc22   2006007005

British Library Cataloguing in Publication Data is available.

This book is included in the *African American Experience*
database from Greenwood Electronic Media. For more
information, visit www.africanamericanexperience.com.

Library of Congress Catalog Card Number: 2006007005
ISBN: 0–313–33686–5
ISSN: 1540–4900

First published in 2006

Greenwood Press, 88 Post Road West, Westport, CT 06881
An imprint of Greenwood Publishing Group, Inc.
www.greenwood.com

Printed in the United States of America

The paper used in this book complies with the
Permanent Paper Standard issued by the National
Information Standards Organization (Z39.48–1984).

10 9 8 7 6 5 4 3 2 1

CONTENTS

CONTENTS

Photo essay follows page 72.

SERIES FOREWORD

In response to high school and public library needs, Greenwood developed this distinguished series of full-length biographies specifically for student use. Prepared by field experts and professionals, these engaging biographies are tailored for high school students who need challenging yet accessible biographies. Ideal for secondary school assignments, the length, format and subject areas are designed to meet educators' requirements and students' interests.

Greenwood offers an extensive selection of biographies spanning all curriculum related subject areas including social studies, the sciences, literature and the arts, history and politics, as well as popular culture, covering public figures and famous personalities from all time periods and backgrounds, both historic and contemporary, who have made an impact on American and/or world culture. Greenwood biographies were chosen based on comprehensive feedback from librarians and educators. Consideration was given to both curriculum relevance and inherent interest. The result is an intriguing mix of the well known and the unexpected, the saints and sinners from long-ago history and contemporary pop culture. Readers will find a wide array of subject choices from fascinating crime figures like Al Capone to inspiring pioneers like Margaret Mead, from the greatest minds of our time like Stephen Hawking to the most amazing success stories of our day like J. K. Rowling.

While the emphasis is on fact, not glorification, the books are meant to be fun to read. Each volume provides in-depth information about the subject's life from birth through childhood, the teen years, and adulthood. A thorough account relates family background and education, traces

personal and professional influences, and explores struggles, accomplish-
ments, and contributions. A timeline highlights the most significant life
events against a historical perspective. Bibliographies supplement the
reference value of each volume.

INTRODUCTION

On August 28, 1963, under a sizzling hot sun in Washington, D.C., more than 200,000 people engulfed the area around the Lincoln Memorial—blacks and whites, young and old, the largest reform demonstration in American history.

On the steps a short distance from the great, brooding statue of the nation's sixteenth president, the "Great Emancipator," the last speaker of the day stepped to the microphone to address the mammoth crowd and a television and radio audience that reached into the millions. Short, stocky, dressed in a black suit, he was the son and grandson of preachers, descendants of slaves freed in the time of Lincoln and the Civil War. He was the man around whom much of the Civil Rights movement in the United States had turned—Dr. Martin Luther King, Jr.

His road to this moment had not been long; after all, he was only 34 years old. But it had been one of momentous times that tugged at the limits of both human cruelty and heroism. It was a time when once again the people of the United States came face to face with its age-old problem of race relations. If human slavery as an institution had been crushed by the Civil War, many legal and social freedoms of black individuals had not yet been achieved. This enormous crowd over which King now looked was here to proclaim that the time had come.

If fateful occurrences had not intervened, he would likely have followed his father as a long-term pastor at a church. Or, more likely, given his intellectual bent, he might have accepted a teaching position at a major university. But the young preacher from Atlanta, Georgia, who was beginning a pastorate in Montgomery, Alabama, was in history's path in 1955. When local civil rights advocates looked for a leader to head a boycott of Montgomery's bus system, King accepted their calling.

With the gifts of dynamic oratory, energy, imagination, and a sense of mission, King led marches and demonstrations and boycotts across the South. The thousands who marched with him faced legal impediments, violence, and hatred. Through it all, they persevered. They overcame. And now, King, along with fellow civil rights leaders and an extraordinary gathering of people from across the country, were saying yes to this movement for human rights and liberties.

Wandering from his prepared text into the language that he had used in countless churches and auditoriums, King eloquently spoke of a dream:

> I have a dream that one day this nation will rise up and live out the true meaning of its creed: "We hold these truths to be self-evident, that all men are created equal."
>
> I have a dream that one day on the red hills of Georgia, the sons of former slaves and the sons of former slave owners will be able to sit down together at the table of brotherhood.... I have a dream that my four little children will one day live in a nation where they will not be judged by the color of their skin but by the content of their character.
>
> I have a dream today.[1]

To this dream and this cause, he would commit his life.

NOTE

1. "200,000 March for Civil Rights in Orderly Washington Rally; President Sees Gain for Negroes," *New York Times*, August 29, 1963.

TIMELINE OF EVENTS IN THE LIFE OF MARTIN LUTHER KING, JR.

January 15, 1929   Michael King, Jr. is born in Atlanta, Georgia, the son of Michael and Alberta King. The boy will be called M. L. King and then Martin Luther King, Jr.

1944   Leaves Booker T. Washington High School after completing eleventh grade and is admitted to Morehouse College in Atlanta at the age of 15.

February 25, 1948   Is ordained into the Baptist ministry at age 19 and appointed to serve as the associate pastor at Ebenezer Baptist Church in Atlanta.

June 8, 1948   Graduates from Morehouse with a Bachelor of Arts degree in sociology.

September 14, 1948   Enters Crozer Theological Seminary in Chester, Pennsylvania.

May 1951   Graduates from Crozer with a bachelor of divinity degree.

September 1951   Begins studying systematic theology as a graduate student at Boston University.

June 18, 1953   Marries Coretta Scott at her parents' home in Marion, Alabama.

1954   Is appointed pastor of the Dexter Avenue Baptist Church in Montgomery, Alabama.

June 5, 1955   Receives Doctorate of Philosophy in Systematic Theology from Boston University, Boston, Massachusetts.

November 17, 1955	Yolanda Denise, King's first child, is born.
December 1, 1955	Rosa Parks, a seamstress, is arrested in Montgomery, Alabama for refusing to give her seat on a bus to a white passenger in violation of local segregation laws.
December 5, 1955	Blacks begin bus boycott and King is elected president of the Montgomery Improvement Association, an organization created to run the boycott.
November 13, 1956	U.S. Supreme Court rules that bus segregation is illegal.
December 21, 1956	Montgomery buses are desegregated.
January 1957	Forms and becomes president of the Southern Christian Leadership Conference (SCLC) to fight segregation and achieve civil rights.
May 17, 1957	Speaks to a crowd of 15,000 in Washington, D.C.
October 23, 1957	Second child, Martin Luther King III, is born.
June 23, 1958	Meets with President Dwight D. Eisenhower.
February 1959	Visits India for a month to study Mohandas Gandhi's philosophy of nonviolence.
February 1960	Resigns from Dexter Baptist Church and moves with family to Atlanta to serve as co-pastor with his father at Ebenezer Baptist Church and to continue as head of SCLC at its home office.
1960	Lunch counter sit-ins begin in Greensboro, North Carolina.
October 19, 1960	Is arrested at a sit-in in Atlanta.
January 31, 1961	Third child, Dexter, is born.
1961	Congress on Racial Equality (CORE) begins first "Freedom Ride" through the South to protest segregated bus facilities.
October 16, 1961	Meets with President John F. Kennedy to gain his support for the civil rights movement.
July 27, 1962	During protest movement in Albany, Georgia, King is arrested and jailed.
March 28, 1963	Fourth child, Bernice Albertine, is born.
April 12, 1963	Is arrested in Birmingham, Alabama by Police Commissioner Eugene "Bull" Connor for demonstrating without a permit. While incarcerated he writes "Letter from a Birmingham Jail." Arrest marks beginning of desegregation movement in

	Birmingham that gathers worldwide publicity of the force and violence marshaled against the protestors.
May 10, 1963	Agreement is reached in Birmingham to desegregate stores, restaurants, and schools.
June 23, 1963	Leads 125,000 people on a "Freedom Walk" in Detroit, Michigan.
August 28, 1963	Speaks at the March on Washington for Jobs and Freedom at the Lincoln Memorial, where he delivers to a quarter of a million people his famous "I Have a Dream" speech.
January 3, 1964	Appears on the cover of *Time* magazine as its Man of the Year.
July 2, 1964	Attends the signing ceremony of the Civil Rights Act of 1964 at the White House.
December 10, 1964	At age 35, is awarded the Nobel Peace Prize, the youngest person to be given the award.
February 2, 1965	Is arrested in Selma, Alabama, during a voting rights demonstration.
January 22, 1966	Moves into a Chicago slum tenement to attract attention to the living conditions of the poor.
June 7, 1966	After civil rights leader James Meredith is shot and wounded, joins Floyd McKissick and Stokely Carmichael to resume Meridith's "March Against Fear" from Memphis to Jackson, Mississippi.
July 10, 1966	After addressing more than 50,000 people at Soldier Field in Chicago, leads the marchers to City Hall, where he posts demands on the door of Mayor Richard J. Daley for an end to discrimination in housing, employment, and schools in the city.
March 17–25, 1967	Leads march from Selma, Alabama, to Montgomery for voting rights.
April 4, 1967	At New York City's Riverside Church, makes passionate statement against the Vietnam War.
November 27, 1967	Announces the inception of the Poor People's Campaign, focusing on jobs and freedom for the poor of all races.
March 28, 1968	Leads striking sanitation workers in a march in Memphis, Tennessee. The march erupts in violence.

April 3, 1968	Leads another march with sanitation workers; at a rally at Mason Temple, King delivers his last speech, "I've Been to the Mountaintop."
April 4, 1968	While standing on the balcony of the Lorraine Motel in Memphis, is shot and killed.
April 9, 1968	Funeral in Atlanta.

Chapter 1

SWEET AUBURN

Martin Luther King, Jr. once noted that his father and brother were both preachers and that his grandfather and great-grandfather on his mother's side of the family had also been preachers. Preaching, he mused, seemed to be his life's only course.

He was born on January 15, 1929 in an upstairs room of a modest, middle-class home on Atlanta's Auburn Avenue, a short distance from one of the most respected and influential churches in the black community—Ebenezer Baptist Church.

He was the second child and first son of Michael King, Sr. and Alberta Christine Williams King. The couple named the boy after the father, but throughout his youth he was simply called "M. L." by the family. Later, both the father and the son changed their names, adopting "Martin Luther" after the German religious leader whose writings and work launched the Protestant Reformation, the great religious revolt of the sixteenth century.

A LINEAGE OF PREACHING

In Martin Luther King, Jr.'s veins flowed the blood of generations of fiery black preachers, figures around whom congregations turned for word of redemption, the affirmation that the crosses of injustice and prejudice that plagued their days would be made right by God's power. The family's strong religious roots were from rural Georgia, and its preachers went as far back as the days of slavery before the Civil War.

Willis Williams, Martin Luther King's great-grandfather, was a slave and a fire-and-brimstone preacher in the Shiloh Baptist Church in

Greene County, Georgia, about 70 miles east of Atlanta. Shiloh's congregation in the 1840s numbered nearly 80 members, of which more than 20 were slaves. After the Civil War, the Williams family and other blacks organized their own Baptist church, as did many other black families and communities across the South.

Influenced by the powerful oratory of his father, A. D. Williams, King's grandfather, learned the cadences and rhythms of black preaching, learned how to turn the stories and parables of the Scripture into personal lessons, and learned how to whip up the emotions of his listeners into a feverish common connection with the Almighty.

A. D. Williams began his own itinerant ministry in the late 1880s and early 1890s. With other many rural natives of Georgia, Williams migrated to a growing civic center of black life—Atlanta. By 1894, Williams had made such a mark on the black community that he was asked to be the pastor of Ebenezer Baptist Church, then one of the many very small black churches in the city.

His charismatic oratory drew a steadily growing congregation of poor and working class black Atlantans. Foremost a preacher, Williams was also a proponent of social change and active politically in various religious and activist organizations such as the National Association for the Advancement of Colored People (NAACP). He was also involved in establishing the high school that his grandson would later attend.

Under his able leadership, Ebenezer grew to nearly 750 members by 1913. After changing the location of the church on two separate occasions, Williams persuaded the congregation to purchase a lot on the corner of Auburn Avenue and Jackson Street and announced plans to raise funds for a new building that would include seats for more than 1,000 worshippers. The main part of the building was completed in 1922. From a congregation of 13 black individuals at the time of its founding in 1886, Ebenezer Baptist Church was now poised to become a major religious and social force in the middle of a burgeoning population of blacks in Atlanta

At the same time A. D. Williams was establishing Ebenezer Baptist Church as one of the most influential in Atlanta's black community, his only child, Alberta, was achieving an impressive education. A graduate of Atlanta's Spelman Seminary, she also attended Hampton Normal and Industrial Institute in Virginia, where she received a teaching certificate in 1924. When she returned to Atlanta from Virginia, Alberta began to see regularly a young, aspiring preacher. His name was Michael King.

The eldest of nine children, son of a sharecropper, and a member of the Floyd Chapel Baptist Church, King, like Alberta's father, also harbored burning passions about racial injustice. King had watched his father and mother work the fields for little pay and no respect. Increasingly, the work left them physically debilitated and relatively powerless to do anything to improve their lives. He watched the insults and the harsh treatment of his family and others living a hardscrabble life and saw the frustration and anger take a terrible toll on their lives. He later talked about a lynching in his neighborhood and talked about his own father living in the woods for a time on the run from a vigilante group bent on stringing him up.

When he listened intently to preachers and activists in Atlanta decry the legal and social subjugation under which the black community existed, he gained an increasing determination to break out of the poverty and discrimination that he saw all around him and to make a difference. Gradually, throughout his teenage years, Michael King decided to become a minister. Despite his lack of educational opportunities, the barely literate King gained assistance toward his goal from the ministers in his church. Recognizing his zeal and passion, they encouraged him in his reading, encouraged him to seek an education, and helped him hone his natural talent of speaking before the congregation.

And now, during his courtship of Alberta, the Williams family enthusiastically supported Michael's ministerial aspirations. They helped him begin studies at Bryant Preparatory School. After his work at Bryant and after serving as pastor of several small churches in Atlanta, King began a three-year degree program at the Morehouse School of Religion in 1926.

In June of that year Michael and Alberta announced their engagement at a Sunday service at Ebenezer Church and on Thanksgiving Day 1926 they exchanged wedding vows. After the marriage, the two moved into the Williams home on Auburn Avenue, the main street of Atlanta's African American business district. It was in this home that Martin Luther King, Jr., along with his brother Alfred Daniel (A. D.) and sister Willie Christine were born.

In 1926, Williams asked his new son-in-law and young preacher to serve as an assistant pastor at Ebenezer. A large man well over 200 pounds, a dynamic speaker with a commanding presence, known throughout most of his life as "Daddy King," King, Sr. made an increasingly strong impression and developed close relationships with the congregation at Ebenezer.

When Williams passed away in 1931, King, Sr. replaced him as pastor of Ebenezer. Not only did King grow the membership of the church substantially in the coming years, he became in his own right an influential preacher. Later in his life, Martin Luther King, Jr. spoke of his father as a dynamic influence in his life, a man radiating strength and confidence, unafraid of facing tough challenges, especially in his dealings with the white community. It was his father, King, Jr., said, who urged him at an early age not to accept lamely the unjust prejudices and social and legal conventions that held down the black race in America. In a 1940 address to a Baptist gathering, King, Sr. challenged the religious community to stand up for true Christian democracy, the Christianity that taught love and equality, not division and discord, the Christianity that called for inclusion not alienation.

The younger King was amazed throughout his life that his father had not been attacked physically. As president of the NAACP in Atlanta and as a strong proponent of social reform, he was certainly an obvious target for violence. Many social reform advocates and fellow preachers had been victims of racial assaults over the years; some had lost their lives. Yet, this strong and challenging voice from the pulpit at Ebenezer continued to stoke the growing restlessness in the black community for change and continued to serve as an example to his family.

A BOYHOOD ON AUBURN AVENUE

"Sweet Auburn" it was called, the one-mile long, and two-block wide area where thousands of blacks, many former slaves and their descendants, had settled in downtown Atlanta. The growth of the area was hastened after a violent city-wide race riot shortly after the turn of the century. In late September 1906, sparked by unsubstantiated rumors against blacks, large crowds of whites assaulted blacks in several Atlanta neighborhoods. Fearing for their lives, large numbers of blacks fled the city; others gathered together in the Auburn Avenue area as a means of self-protection, attempting to isolate themselves from the racial hatred and violence in the security of their own race. Much like the self-contained area of Harlem in New York, it became over the years a kind of safe haven and cultural entity for thousands of blacks.

John Wesley Dobbs, a black civic leader in the city, reputedly coined the name "Sweet Auburn." Considered by many the "Godfather of black business" in Atlanta, Dobbs started the Atlanta Negro Voters league and helped increase the number of black voters from less than 2,000 in 1940 to more than 22,000 in the early 1950's. He lived with his wife and six daughters on Auburn Avenue, a few blocks from the home of the Kings. Martin Luther King, Jr. could often be found in his young days playing Monopoly on the kitchen floor of Dobbs's home with some of the Dobbs clan. Dobbs's grandson, Maynard Jackson, Jr., would in 1970 become the city's first elected black mayor.

Sweet Auburn was a place where blacks could own businesses, get a good education at nearby black colleges, and prosper. The neighborhood was electric, alive with black-owned nightclubs such as the Royal Peacock and the Top Hat Club, where musical greats such as Cab Calloway, Bessie Smith, Ray Charles, and Duke Ellington performed. There were big churches, fancy restaurants, clean hotels, the Prince Hall Masonic Building, and a string of businesses, from beauty salons to funeral parlors to the Sweet Auburn Curb Market.

In the early 1920s, Sweet Auburn boasted over 100 black-owned enterprises. A quick stroll throughout the neighborhood would take you past the large and the small, from mom-and-pop eateries such as Hawk's Dinette and Ma Sutton's to the giant Atlanta Life Insurance Corporation, the first black-owned life insurance company. It was home to the first black daily newspaper, the Atlanta *Daily World*, and the first black-owned radio station in the United States, WERD.

In this dynamic community, mostly devoid of the super-rich or the extremely poor, an area of relatively low crime where most citizens were closely connected to their churches and their families, Martin Luther King, Jr. spent his early years. Beginning his education in 1935 at the Yonge Street Elementary School and then at the David T. Howard Elementary School through the sixth grade, he was not a precocious youngster academically, although he seemed to appreciate the power of language. After hearing the especially effective oratorical talents of a visiting minister, Martin announced to his family that one day he would employ big words. Indeed, he began to practice, at times startling his teachers with such word concoctions as "Cogitating with the cosmic universe, I surmise that my physical equilibrium is organically quiescent."[1]

As a minister's son, King's life, not surprisingly, revolved almost exclusively around the church. He grew up in a household where all members regularly read the Bible, sang hymns, and prayed aloud. Along with his brother and sister, Martin was expected to memorize Bible verses and recite them.

Not only was his father a minister of a growing and influential church, his mother trained the Ebenezer Choir and was the church's organist. So talented was Alberta King that various Baptist groups in Georgia asked her to perform and she began organizing annual musical performances of Ebenezer's choirs. His mother encouraged Martin as early as age four to sing with various church groups.

"The church has always been a second home for me," he later wrote. "As far back as I can remember, I was in church every Sunday.... My best friends were in Sunday School, and it was the Sunday School that helped me to build my capacity for getting along with people."[2]

As Martin listened not only to his father but other preachers at Ebenezer, he could feel the emotionalism at work among the congregation, moved as it was by the rhythms of the gospel belted out in thunderous beats, with the clapping and shouting at the preacher to raise the pulsating level on to even greater heights. At Ebenezer, as at many other black churches across the country, this was a religion that was mountain-moving, tough, in which every member of the congregation, calling out "Amen" and, swinging to the spirit, had a part, regardless of their everyday circumstances. In the church pews was a democracy before God and it had nothing to do with rich or poor. King could see the passion; he could recognize its spirit, but he was uncomfortable with it. To the boy, it seemed vaguely disturbing, the masses in the crowd giving themselves over to an enthusiasm that he did not quite understand. He admitted some time later that much of the emotionalism embarrassed him.

King joined the church at the age of five when a guest evangelist from Virginia encouraged converts to come forward. When his sister made her move to join, Martin was not far behind. Later, when thinking back on this moment and also on the time he was baptized, he admitted that the rituals had little to do with his religious belief or conviction but almost everything to do with keeping up with his sister.

Later in his life, King talked about the gnawing doubts about religious messages and impulses that were part of his everyday life. With the constant expectations, not only by his family but others in the community, that he assume the proper role of the religious son, instead he found himself increasingly dubious about some of the biblical stories and churchly practices. "I guess I accepted biblical studies uncritically until I was about twelve years old," King wrote. "But this uncritical attitude could not last long, for it was contrary to the very nature of my being. I had always been the questioning and precocious type. At the age of thirteen, I shocked my Sunday school class by denying the bodily resurrection of Jesus. Doubts began to spring forth unrelentingly."[3]

King later looked back on his childhood with much fondness—a relatively comfortable middle-class existence within a caring and responsible family and constant personal encouragement and support. King's father tended to be a strong disciplinarian, occasionally whipping Martin and his brother, A. D. Nevertheless, the father's stern discipline was tempered by his wife's more gentle nature. "We talked a lot about the future of the kids," King, Sr. later said, "and she was able to understand that even when

I got very upset with them, it was only because I wanted them to be strong and able and happy."[4]

His parents rarely argued, and the boy could see the strong bonds that united them. Because of the congenial, if busy, atmosphere in his home, he said later, he tended to see the world in more optimistic ways and to value human relationships.

On May 18, 1941, during a Woman's Day program at Ebenezer, Jennie Williams, Martin's grandmother, died of a heart attack. The death of his grandmother occurred while young Martin, against the wishes of his parents, had sneaked off to watch a parade. An avalanche of guilt swept over the young boy, startling in intensity and length. So upset did the 12-year-old King become over the death and the connection that he made in his mind with his attendance at the parade, that he became increasingly moody and depressed. If he had not gone to the parade, he believed, his beloved grandmother would not have died. Burdened by grief and remorse, King, at one point, leaped out of the second-floor window of his house.

During the weeks following the death of his grandmother and his traumatic reaction, both his father and mother patiently spoke with him at length about personal immortality. It was at this time, he said later, that he became a strong believer in an afterlife.

His parents did not isolate the youngster. He took a number of part-time jobs, delivering the *Atlanta Journal* as young as eight years old, and taking on other odd jobs and manual labor well into his teens. In September 1940, following his grade school years, he entered the Laboratory High School of Atlanta University, a progressive private school that appealed to black residents who could afford the cost and who wished to keep their children out of the extremely crowded public schools. Martin completed two years, after which the school closed in 1942. His grades were generally good, although he did fail social studies.

He continued his studies at the public Booker T. Washington High School. In his second year, he won an oratory contest that gave him the opportunity to represent the school in a statewide contest in Dublin, Georgia. The 14-year-old boy was now beginning to display the skills in public speaking that would later propel him into his future career and work.

It was on the way back from the Dublin speaking contest that King experienced first-hand the kind of senseless, painful humiliation against which his father and grandfather and others in his family had been speaking out against for many years. The white bus driver cursed King and his fellow black students for attempting to sit in seats reserved for white passengers. Faced with a difficult situation, the speech coach asked the students to give in to the demand to avoid retaliation. Years later, King was still haunted by the injustice. In an interview in 1965, he said that those moments on the bus made him the angriest he had ever been.

The speech that the youngster delivered in Dublin, Georgia was entitled "The Negro and the Constitution." In it he said, "We cannot be truly Christian people so long as we flaunt the central teachings of Jesus: brotherly love and the Golden Rule."[5]

THE ISSUE OF COLOR

In Martin Luther King's youth, black Americans still had a long climb toward equality. Even though several generations had passed since the Civil War, a large segment of the population, because of their color, remained isolated, poor, and with opportunities so limited as to stifle even the most energetic and talented.

For the black community in Atlanta, as with black communities across the country, much of American society was off limits. Housing in the better-developed sections of town was impossible. Schools and churches had either white or black congregations. If a black individual went downtown, the restaurants and lunch counters in department stores were off-limits, as were theaters and even public libraries.

On public conveyances such as buses and trains, blacks were separated from whites, as they were in public courtrooms and other official buildings. Even more dispiriting and degrading were the signs at water fountains and swimming pools, elevators, and other public places indicating "Whites Only." Blacks had to pay taxes but in many cases did not have the right to vote. From the earliest days of his childhood, Martin learned limitations rather than possibilities. When he was six years old, a white friend suddenly vanished from his life, prohibited by his family from socializing any longer with a black boy. He recognized, even at a very early age, that the social system was overpowering and unfair.

He later remembered not being able to go swimming until the YMCA built a segregated pool. He remembered not being able to enter most of the public parks, or eat at a downtown lunch counter, or attend most movie theaters, or go to any of the best schools.

Nevertheless, unlike many other black youths, King had throughout his young life watched his father refuse to be muscled into acceptance of the degrading system. He might have been forced to endure it; but he never accepted it. In his emerging views on racial discrimination, young Martin had a role model.

Daddy King talked over many dinners about the need to challenge the system. He went out of his way to ride in "Whites Only" elevators. The young Martin remembered an incident in a shoe store when his father refused to move to the back of the room to be served. "This was the first time I had seen Dad so furious," King later wrote. "That experience revealed to me at a very early age that my father had not adjusted to the system, and he played a great part in shaping my conscience. I still remember walking down the street beside him as he muttered, 'I don't care how long I have to live with this system, I will never accept it.' "[6]

He refused to allow his children to attend theaters that were segregated, with blacks sitting in the rear. He refused to ride city buses after witnessing a brutal attack on several blacks. In 1939, fed up with political discrimination, he led several hundred Atlanta Negroes on a voting rights march to City Hall. When the elder King was stopped for a traffic violation on one occasion, the policeman referred to him as a "boy." Indignant, the strapping King, Sr. pointed to Martin and said, "This is a boy. I'm a man, and until you call me one, I will not listen to you."[7]

With his social and political influence growing as the pastor of a respected church, King never skirted the issues of racial equality; indeed, he headed the Atlanta Civic and Political League and the Atlanta Baptist Ministers Union, organizations that worked vigorously to register eligible black voters and to help in other civic causes. King, Sr. also became a leading figure in the Atlanta branch of the NAACP, which won a legal battle to equalize the salaries of white and black teachers.

Young Martin also remembered the patient guidance of his mother in confronting the evils of segregation. She talked to him about the history of slavery and the painful attempts by blacks throughout the years to assert their rights. She told him about the evolving system of segregation that stood defiantly in the way of progress for the black race. She told him that that most important force in his life must be his own sense of self, the image of his own person as one of equality and importance—that his life mattered as much as any other.

Following his completion of the eleventh grade in Booker T. Washington High School in the spring of 1944, King had an opportunity to skip the twelfth grade and to enroll in Morehouse College, the institution from which both his grandfather and father had graduated. With large numbers of young black men serving in the armed forces during World War II, Morehouse lacked the usual numbers of incoming freshmen. The school opened its doors to aspiring students who had completed the eleventh grade and who were able to pass a special entrance examination. Although King's grades throughout grade school and high school had not been exemplary, he did manage to pass the test. Encouraged by his family, King decided to enroll.

In the summer of 1944, King traveled to Simsbury, Connecticut, with about 100 other students to work on a tobacco farm for the summer to help pay college expenses. It was the first time the 15-year-old King had left Atlanta and his family for any extended length of time.

From the Connecticut tobacco farm, King wrote to his father in June 1944 that he was having a good time, working hard, eating well, and that he had become the religious leader of the young group in the Sunday religious service. He also talked about race. "On our way here," he wrote, "we saw some things I had never anticipated to see. After we passed Washington there was no discrimination at all and the white people here are very nice. We go to any place we want to and sit any where we want to."[8]

On his return trip by train to Atlanta, King later remembered the feelings of anger and humiliation he felt when he arrived in Washington, D.C. It was there that blacks on the train had to congregate on a segregated car for the ride into the South. The trip to Connecticut reinforced in the youngster's mind all that his family, his friends, and his own eyes had taught him in Altanta—that segregation was an affront to the dignity of the black race and must be overcome.

NOTES

1. Marshall Frady, *Martin Luther King, Jr.* (New York, Viking, 2002), p. 13.

2. Clayborne Carson, ed., *The Papers of Martin Luther King, Jr.*, vol. 1, *Called to Serve* (Berkeley: University of California Press, 1992), p. 361.

3. Carson, p. 361.

4. Martin Luther King, Sr., with Clayton Riley, *Daddy King: An Autobiography* (New York: William Morrow, 1980), pp. 130–31.

5. Carson, p. 110.

6. Martin Luther King, Jr., *Stride Toward Freedom* (New York: Harper and Brothers, 1958), p. 19.

7. King, Jr., p. 20.

8. Carson, p. 112.

Chapter 2

LEARNING YEARS

MOREHOUSE

In September 1944, Martin Luther King, Jr., age 15, entered Morehouse College, one of the preeminent black institutions of higher education in the South. The roots of the school went back to the early days after the Civil War when a group of former slaves formed a group called the Augusta Institute. From its founding, the school's purpose was to prepare black men for the ministry and teaching.

It was at Morehouse that King would meet one of the individuals whose influence on his life was monumental—Benjamin Mays. Mays had become president of the college in 1940 and had already made a strong mark.

The son of former slaves in South Carolina, Mays had, through grit and determination, overcome innumerable hurdles of class and race. From his beginnings as a dirt-poor laborer picking cotton, he had managed to find his way to the state of Maine, where he worked his way through Bates College to graduate with honors. His educational road led to Chicago, where he was awarded a Ph.D. in the University of Chicago's School of Religion. Mays taught for a time at Morehouse and at South Carolina State College and, from 1934 to 1940, he served as dean of the Howard University School of Religion. Under his leadership Howard rose to a position of distinction among schools of religion.

In professional stature one of the towering black educators in the United States, Mays challenged Morehouse students to refuse the status quo, to fight for the rights of the poor and disenfranchised, and to use their knowledge gained at Morehouse to struggle for the dignity of the black community. Mays traveled to Europe and Asia on a number of occasions and once spoke personally with Mohandas Gandhi in India. A powerful speaker and a man of unrelenting drive, Mays also published a number of books on religion and social change. As King progressed through Morehouse, Mays, in both his personal bearing and his philosophical beliefs, would help shape the life of the youngster from Sweet Auburn.

One of the first classmates King encountered, Walter McCall, was as poor as Martin was relatively privileged. To keep afloat financially, he worked as a barber in the basement of one of Morehouse's student halls, cutting hair for a dime. Even though King himself had little money at Morehouse, McCall had far less and, on one occasion, when King received a haircut and realized he did not have a dime on him, McCall exploded. The two wrestled on the grass outside, drawing a crowd. Although smaller, King earned McCall's respect in the skirmish and the two became close friends. Others began to call them "Mac and Mike."

Mac was as skeptical of some religious beliefs and trappings as King was, and when they attended church together they sat in the balcony, as if to emphasize their divergent beliefs. By this time King had decided not to become a minister. He felt no calling for it. His inner drive told him to rebel against the strong wishes of his family, especially his father, that he must follow in the footsteps of his preacher forbearers. By the time he had settled into his classroom routine at Morehouse, he had made a tenetative decision to become a lawyer.

King lived at home during his school years at Morehouse and did not join a fraternity. But he gained many new friends and had a lively social life, at the expense of studious attention to his classes. The chunky, five-foot seven-inch tall King loved to dance and was inclined early on to mingle easily with girls. He joined a number of campus groups including the sociology club, glee club, ministers' union, and the Morehouse chapter of the NAACP, and he played basketball at the Butler Street YMCA. Not surprisingly, his natural aptitude for public speaking assured his place as a member of the debating club. During his sophomore year, he won second prize in an oratorical contest. He also became a member of the student council.

King was exhilarated by the give and take at Morehouse, by the freedom to get some of his ideas that he had suppressed at home out in the open. Although protected and nurtured in the family, he had also, as the son of a minister, felt trapped by convention and by expectation. He later looked back on the experience as opening up a new world. "There was a freer atmosphere at Morehouse," King said.[1]

May's sermons excited King almost immediately. Angular-faced, with touches of silver at his temples, the schoolmaster exuded enthusiasm for learning, especially when he gathered the boys of Morehouse for his lectures on most Tuesdays. One of his students later remembered: "Mays got to us through those Tuesday chapel sessions. He told us, 'Yes, there is segregation, but your mind is free. Your job is to cultivate your mind to its fullest extent. Now segregation is a reality, but it is not an excuse. What is important is to make your mind work.' "[2]

Mays once wrote that from his earliest days in the cotton fields of South Carolina he had a searing desire to learn, 'vaguely, yet ardently, I longed to *know*, for I sensed that knowledge could set me free."[3]

And now, from Mays, the young King began to see what Mays had seen—the power of learning and the practical strength of ideas. Through education was liberation.

At Morehouse, King also admired a young professor and friend of the King family who had recently received his doctorate from Yale University. George E. Kelsey, a professor of religion, later remembered King as a student whose eagerness increased as the subject matter became challenging and controversial. When he talked in his class about the problem of race as the greatest moral dilemma confronting the United States, Kelsey saw King's eyes light up and a smile begin to crease his face.

In closely tying religious teaching to social problems and obligations, in relieving King from the rigors of dealing with a strict Baptist fundamentalism and freeing his mind to explore alternative notions to his earlier religious training, Morehouse led King through an intellectual journey. The journey would have an ending that even he might not have foreseen. This was a religion with a social purpose, and the young student increasingly saw himself at the pulpit. The more he heard teachers such as Mays and Kelsey, the more he began to reconsider his rebellious reatreat from his preaching forbearers.

In July 1946, the issue of race exploded in nightmarish incidents near Atlanta following a local election. A man named Macio Snipes, a World War II veteran and the only black individual to cast a vote in his district in Taylor County, Georgia, was surrounded the following day by four white men and shot to death. Shortly thereafter, two black couples driving in their cars near Monroe, Georgia, were stopped and shot by a contingent of 20 men. When King read about the murders in the *Atlanta Constitution* he was not only outraged by the senseless and murderous rage against black people but also angered by the stance taken by the newspaper. While lamenting the loss of life, the newspaper's editorialists maintained their opposition to any legislation that would place such mob violence under the jurisdiction of the federal government. The state, insisted the editorialists, was fully equipped to deal with any matters of law and order at the local level.

King was incensed by the situation. Ready to begin his junior year, the Morehouse student fired off a letter to the *Constitution*. The paper published it on August 6, 1946. King opened with an attack on those who roar the loudest about racial purity and the dangers of race mixing. Those attacks, King insisted, were simply dust kicked up to obscure the real motivations behind such violence—race prejudice. He wrote, "We want and are entitled to the basic rights and opportunities of American citizens: The right to earn a living at work for which we are fitted by training and ability; equal opportunities in education, health, recreation, and similar public services; the right to vote; equality before the law; some of the same courtesy and good manners that we ourselves bring to all human relations."[4]

King's father said later that it was not until the *Atlanta Constitution* published the letter that either he or Martin's mother had an indication that Martin was headed for greatness. When the boy took the independent step to channel his beliefs and frustrations about the race issue directly to the public, it now became clear that their son at Morehouse was no ordinary college junior.

The elder King had always wanted both of his sons to follow his own steps in the ministry, perhaps even joining him at Ebenezer. Martin's brother, A. D. made a short effort to attend Morehouse but soon dropped out, although he did later follow a ministerial career. Martin's early aspirations while in college to become either a physician or a lawyer must have hurt King, Sr., but he also accepted the counsel of his wife that the children must be free to make their own choices. King's older sister, Christine, was also on an academic path, studying economics at Spelman College. She would later enter Columbia University for graduate work.

By the time King was 17, during his junior year at Morehouse, he made the critical decision—he would become a minister. Looking back years later, he remembered the decision as something other than a lightening bolt of inspiration or a heavenly hand that had suddenly rested on his shoulder; he remembered it, rather, as "an inner urge to serve humanity." Still with an aversion to the joyously riotous style of worship he had seen in most black churches, he strove toward a "rational" approach, he said, to be a minister whose power would be "a respectable force for ideas, even social protest."[5]

Although uncomfortable with some of literal beliefs held so firmly by most members of the black church, King's roots in the traditions and forms of the church held fast. He loved the music and was himself an able singer. He admired the history of those who had created out of the experience of slavery a community of people who struggled together. He admired the leadership of many of the religious figures, from his father to men such as the Reverend William Holmes Borders of Atlanta's Wheat Street Church, a powerful speaker with impressive academic credentials, who became the first black preacher in Atlanta to host a radio program. As a young teenager, King often sat with his ear pressed to the radio speaker listening to the oratory of Reverend Borders. Yes, he would become a preacher, one who would try to make a social and political difference.

When he told his parents his decision, his overjoyed father seized the moment and immediately told the Ebenezer congregation of the news, that his son had been called to pastoral service. In the tradition of Ebenezer and other black Baptist clergy, Reverend King scheduled an immediate trial sermon to be delivered by his son at the church.

On a Sunday afternoon, lines of Ebenezer members began to fill the church basement where such introductory sermons were usually held. It was clear early on that the space was not nearly adequate to hear the preacher's son make his inaugural sermon in the church that had already been so much a part of his life. Reverend King hurriedly directed the hundreds upstairs to the main sanctuary.

In preparing for the sermon, King took much of the text from a published sermon of Harry Emerson Fosdick of Riverside Church in New York. With the congregation in rapt attention, Martin stood at the pulpit where both his grandfather and father had been revered. Without the commanding physical presence of his strapping father, the son, nevertheless, filled the hall with his surprisingly mellifluent voice, his cadences and word command seeming like those of a much older and more experienced preacher, his baritone voice clear, powerful, and reassuring. The platform was his and he soared.

Following the service, the congregation, at the call of Reverend King, took steps necessary to license young Martin as an Ebenezer preacher. He became officially an associate pastor of the church. And then, in February 1948, during his final year at Morehouse, he was ordained as a minister.

His senior year at Morehouse seemed almost triumphant. King was now already a minister, something of a campus celebrity. He became a member of an interracial group from the various white and black colleges in the Atlanta area that met monthly to discuss social issues. It was this group that enabled King to test his mantle in a setting outside black circles. It was this group that helped scramble King's natural tendency to hate all whites. He later said that these encounters were invaluable in softening his resentment and looking to a spirit of cooperation, rather than total confrontation. He began to see himself playing a part in breaking down the antipathy between the races and seeking ways to find common ground.

He graduated with a degree in sociology in June 1948. On the same day, his sister Christine received her own bachelor's degree from Spelman.

Although King's father did not encourage Martin to continue his education toward a graduate degree, the young preacher decided to leave Atlanta for a time and to enroll in Crozer Theological Seminary in Pennsylvania. Life now was exciting and rewarding. At 19, he had much more to learn, many young girls to date, and much living ahead before settling down as a minister. In the fall of 1948, King traveled north to the small industrial town of Chester, Pennsylania.

CROZER

Crozer Theological Seminary traced its beginnings to the period of the Civil War. Near Philadelphia, the main building, originally constructed in 1857, served as a United States army hospital during the war. A large proportion of the nearly 100 students at Crozer were white.

At 19 years old, King was younger than most of his classmates. Although his father was not particularly pleased that his son had decided to attend a school over 800 miles north made up mostly of whites, he was determined to do what he could to help ease the transition. He contacted an old friend named J. Pious Barbour, the pastor of Calvary Baptist Church. When King arrived in Chester, Barbour was there to greet him.

A large, barrel-chested man, Barbour was very much like King, Sr. in both appearance and bearing. King was a frequent guest for dinner in the Barbour home from his earliest days in Chester. There, along with the home cooking of Mrs. Olee Barbour, King enjoyed much conversation about not only the courses he was taking at Crozer but about activities in the black community and church. Barbour often invited other blacks in King's class to join in the conversations.

In an early letter home to his mother, King talked about his studies and about meeting a girl he used to date in Atlanta. He wrote: "Also I met a fine chick in Phila who has gone wild over the old boy. Since Barbor [sic] told the members of his church that my family was rich, the girls are running me down. Of course, I don't ever think about them I am to [sic] busy studying. I eat dinner at the Barbors home quite often. He is full of fun, and he has one of the best minds of anybody I have ever met."[6]

Through Barbour, King maintained his connections with the black church. He taught Sunday School at Calvary Baptist, and, on occasion, preached. Thus, as King began to study closely the great philosophers and theologians, Barbour and his church helped forge a continuity in King's evolving view of the world. King would accept much of the teaching to which he was exposed at Crozer, but he would also cling to the traditions and spirit of his preacher forbearers.

Crozer was the first school attended by King that was not segregated. When Walter McCall joined King at Crozer to begin the second semester, he was astonished at the change in his friend's work habits. Here at Crozer, King felt a challenge to compete with the white students that was compelling; many nights he got little sleep, reading with great purpose. Here, the carefree, haphazard routines were gone; now, there was a regimen. As he read the works of Plato, John Locke, Emanuel Kant, Reinhold Niebuhr, and those of his namesake, Martin Luther, he geared up to take whatever Crozer was able to deal out. The mediocre grades at Morehouse gave way to marks that would propel him to the head of the class.

When he first began work at Crozer, King felt burdened by self-consciousness, sensing more than ever before the need to impress the majority white population. He was acutely careful of being on time for his classes, kept himself impeccably groomed and dressed and his room spotless, and affected a degree of seriousness that was not naturally at his core. As he developed friendships and became much more at ease, the affectations wore away. He could laugh and party with ease. At times he drank beer, smoked, and played pool.

He dated often. One of the young women with whom he developed a strong attachment was a white girl of German background whose mother worked for Crozer. As the bond became increasingly serious, Reverend Barbour felt obliged to speak to King about the difficulties that would undoubtedly arise if he persisted in an interracial relationship. How could he possibly return to the South and carry on his duties as a minister while engaged in such a romantic relationship? Although practical, Barbour's advice stunned King. Once again, this question of color plagued his life. Reluctantly, King and the young woman drifted apart.

Much of King's written academic work was shoddy. His papers lacked originality; indeed, much of his writing was merely the compilation of ideas and words taken from books and articles that he failed to identify. In the world of theology, lifting sections of writing from the speeches and sermons of other ministers, both contemporary and long deceased, was a tradition. Ministers heard speeches and read tracts of other writers and ministers and used them freely. This kind of plagiarism in the world of practicing ministers was one thing; in an academic setting it was certainly another.

Nevertheless, King was such an affable and eager student that teachers either looked the other way or did not carefully check his work. The young student continued to receive high marks. Much of the inclination of the faculty to ignore the egregious lack of originality in his written work was unquestionably due to the growing expectation that King was a student of great promise, destined to make a difference.

It was also due to his enormous gift of oratory. So enamored of his speaking did members of the student body become that they filled the chapel to hear his sermons. When word skipped around campus that King was to give a speech, the turnout was always impressive. Here, these students could see early on the characteristics and small details that millions around the world would at a later time see on display—the tucking away of the prepared speech as he reached the podium, as if to say that for him such props were totally unnecessary; the formal, rounded speech pattern with touches of humor; the flourishes of word combinations; the rising and falling of the volume for emphasis, and the increasing crescendo reaching the end.

King became president of the senior class and delivered the valedictory address. He also won an award for the most outstanding student and received a cash fellowship for further graduate study at a university of his choice. He received his Bachelor of Divinity degree.

But King was still not ready to settle down as a minister in Georgia. Sensing that a doctorate degree from a major university would set him apart from most other black ministers, and still flushed with enthusiasm from his successes at Crozer, King decided to use the fellowship and seek a Ph.D. Accepted by several programs including Yale, and Edinburgh in Scotland, he chose the School of Theology at Boston University.

Crozer had awakened his intellectual curiosity and yearning, had given him the impetus to make the crucial decision of his life—to become a minister. Crozer also introduced him to an influence that would shape his social and religious philosophy—the life and ideas of Mohandas Gandhi.

GANDHI AND NONVIOLENT PROTEST

King's father was once asked whether he had seen evidence early on that his son would achieve great distinction. "Heavens no," King, Sr. responded. "He drifted until he connected Christianity to Gandhi."[7]

Born in Gujarat, India in 1869 into a business community family, Mohandas Gandhi studied law in England. At the end of the nineteenth century, he arrived in South Africa on behalf of a client. Gandhi dressed in typical British attire. Nevertheless, while once attempting to travel in the first-class compartment of a train reserved for whites only, he was forcibly removed for violating the segregation policies of the railroad.

Gandhi responded to such injustices by launching a movement for civil rights in South Africa and succeeded in changing some of the laws. When he returned to India in 1915, it was to a hero's welcome. While in South Africa, Gandhi had developed a philosophy for challenging the social and political order through nonviolent protest, a concept of "Soul Force"—nonviolent resistance of conquering through love.

He began to challenge fellow Indians to adopt similar methods to confront their own political and social subjugation by the British in India. In 1920 Gandhi became the leader of the Indian National Congress.

He began to live an ascetic life of prayer, fasting, and meditation. No longer did the studious lawyer dress in the style of whites; he now put on the simple, plain loincloths and robes of an Indian farmer and subsisted on vegetables, fruit juices, and goat's milk. He built an ashram in which everyone in it undertook all of the different jobs, even cleaning the toilet, which according to Indian customs was the job reserved only for the lowest of classes. Even when traveling back to England as head of the Indian National Congress, he continued to wear the plain garments. He drew astonished attention from his diplomatic counterparts and extensive comment from the British press, much of it derisive.

Nevertheless, he did have their attention and he began to speak of the injustices endured by the lower classes of Indian society and the subservient role into which Indian peoples had been reduced by British rule. His call was for Indians to resist British control through nonviolent opposition. Nothing could be gained by forceful revolution, he said, but the yoke of oppression could be lifted by large-scale noncooperation by a united Indian society. He advised Indians to boycott British-made garments. He told them not to attend British universities, as he had done. He told them to refuse to follow customs. The goal was to hurt the British occupiers economically and to overwhelm military might by the sheer force of the numbers of resisters. Through nonviolent protest, Gandhi held, the British would eventually consider violence useless and would eventually leave India. Gandhi became the international symbol of a free India.

As he read of Gandhi's life and philosophy, King was particularly struck by the power that could be unleashed by nonviolent protest. In 1930 Gandhi had called on the Indian population to refuse to pay taxes, particularly the tax on salt. He organized a massive, 24-day march to the sea, in which thousands of Indians followed Gandhi from Ahmedabad to the Arabian Sea. There, he made salt by evaporating seawater. Once again arrested, he was released in 1931 with the British making concessions on their taxing policies.

His "Quit India" crusade helped lead to Indian independence in 1947. He was assassinated a year later by a political enemy.

It was at a lecture at Crozer by A. J. Muste, a well-known American pacifist, where King received his first exposure to the ideas of Gandhi. Much of it resonated positively in his mind as he thought about the racial divide separating his own country, although at first he was skeptical about the possibility of adapting the techniques in the American South.

In 1950 King traveled to Philadelphia to hear a talk given by Mordecai Johnson, president of Howard University. After returning from a visit to India, Johnson spoke admiringly of Gandhi's tactics. His was not a passive philosophy; this was active, loud, disruptive noncooperation. King was beginning to see that boycotts, strikes, protest marches, all grounded in a spirit of justice and love for the oppressor, might actually be effective in challenging racial barriers. So caught up in the speech was King that he bought several books on Gandhi.

He later wrote that Gandhi, by cutting the chain of hatred, lifted the love ethic of Christ to an effective social force. "The Gandhian philosophy of nonviolence," he said, "is the only logical and moral approach to the solution of the race problem in the United States."[8]

At the time of King's death years later, his wallet contained among its contents a small, torn, and fading piece of paper. The handwritten note contained a quote from Gandhi: "In the midst of death, life persists.... In the midst of darkness, light persists." Martin Luther King, in the spirit of Gandhi, was determined to say yes to life and to light.[9]

NOTES

1. Lerone Bennett, Jr., "The Last of the Great Schoolmasters," *Ebony*, September 2004, http://www.findarticles.com/p/articles/mi_m1077/is_11_59/ai_n6172408.

2. Roger Wilkins, "Benjamin Mays," *Nation* (July 21, 2003), p. 28.

3. Wilkins, p. 27.

4. Clayborne Carson, ed., *The Papers of Martin Luther King, Jr.*, vol. 1, *Called to Serve* (Berkeley: University of California Press, 1992), p. 121.

5. Marshall Frady, *Martin Luther King, Jr.* (New York, Viking, 2002), p. 18.

6. Carson, p. 161.

7. "God's Co-Workers for Justice: Address by Billy O. Wireman, President, Queens College Delivered to the Martin Luther King, Jr. Celebration at Belk Chapel, Queens College, Charlotte, N.C., January 19, 1998," *Vital Speeches of the Day*, 3 March 1998, p. 316.

8. "The Martin Luther King, Jr. Papers Project: Biography: Mohandas Karamchand Gandhi (1869–1948)," http://www.stanford.edu/group/King/about_king/encyclopedia/gandhi.htm.

9. "M. K. Gandhi Institute for Nonviolence: About Gandhi," http://www.gandhiinstitute.org/AboutGandhi/index.cfm.

Chapter 3

BOSTON AND CORETTA

In early September 1951, King packed his clothes, stepped into a new green Chevrolet that his father had presented him as a graduation gift, and headed north to continue his education. He entered graduate school at Boston University's School of Theology. Raymond Bean, one of King's favorite professors at Crozer, had graduated from Boston University and told the young student that the school was unusually hospitable to black students.

Nevertheless, if King had temporarily left the segregationist South, he had not in Boston left behind the constant reminders of his race. "I remember very well trying to find a place to live," he said later. "I went into place after place where there were signs that rooms were for rent. They were for rent until they found out I was a Negro, and suddenly they had just been rented."[1]

King finally settled in an apartment near the intersection of Massachusetts and Columbus Avenues, in the heart of a vibrant black area of Boston. It was there that well-dressed patrons gathered in restaurants and jazz halls and where a parade of world-class entertainers played to enthusiastic audiences. "The South End was a different place back then, I must admit," said Myra McAdoo, who befriended King in Boston. "You had Wally's, you had Slades', the Savoy, and the beautiful art deco Hi-Hat jazz club right on the corner. Everyone came there—Count Basie, Duke Ellington, everyone—and people of all backgrounds came from everywhere to hear them. It was, actually, a very progressive area."[2]

John Cartwright, a fellow graduate student, remembered King as "a struggling doctoral student who was a normal guy—even a bit of a playboy. He joked around, he dated—he was a man about town with a new Chevy."[3]

In his studies at Boston University, King was deeply influenced by Dean Walter Muelder and Professor Allen Knight Chalmers, both of whom held strong pacifist beliefs and a fighting spirit for social justice. King did most of his graduate work under L. Harold DeWolf, with whom he developed a strong friendship. He also studied under Edgar S. Brightman. Both DeWolf and Brightman were proponents of a philosophy called "Personalism," an approach to religious philosophy that emphasized that humans were active coworkers with God, a relationship that demonstrated the dignity and worth of all human personality.

"In 1954 I ended my formal training with divergent intellectual forces converging into a positive social philosophy," King wrote later. "One of the main tenets of this philosophy was the conviction that nonviolent resistance was one of the most potent weapons available to oppressed people in their quest for social justice. Interestingly enough, at this time I had merely an intellectual understanding and appreciation of the position, with no firm determination to organize it in a socially effective situation."[4]

King received satisfactory grades at Boston University, even though his papers displayed little originality. Many of King's essays, as well as his dissertation, relied upon words and ideas that he had lifted from other sources without providing citations. As had been the case at Crozer, his teachers, dazzled by his enormous skills in oratory and impressed by his classroom behavior, did not detect the incidents of plagiarism.

King was quickly gaining considerable notice not only within the confines of the university but in numerous outside activities. He organized a Dialectical Society consisting of a dozen theological students who met monthly to discuss philosophical and theological ideas and their application to the racial situation in the United States. King also delivered sermons at local churches, particularly the Twelfth Baptist Church in Roxbury.

As he plunged into the tangled intricacies of philosophical and religious writings and the belief systems of Christianity, Buddhism, Hinduism, and Mohammedanism, and as he considered the philosophical stances of such writers as Hegel, Marx, and Niebuhr, and the outlines of capitalism, communism, and other political philosophies, King emerged with a solidified respect for Gandhi's nonviolent methods of social protest. Pacifism, he believed, was anything but passive, but an active strike against evil by the power of love. Such nonviolent resistance, King was convinced, was both courageous and morally consistent.

King reveled in the bachelor life in Boston, skipping on the weekends from one jazz club to another, hopping from one romance to another. One of his friends sent a friendly warning note to King about his "gallivanting" around town, reminding his friend that he and the others expected big things from him and that the only "element to restrain our expectations bearing fruit" would be King himself.[5]

But the whirl of gallivanting, for which King found time in the midst of his studies, would take a new turn. King's friend John Cartwright later recalled a favorite source for the girls they befriended: "I can't tell you how quickly we all found the New England Conservatory of Music," said Cartwright. "We'd never seen so many talented women in one place."[6]

King met one of those women at the Conservatory. Her name was Coretta Scott and she would change his life.

MARRYING CORETTA

Born on April 27, 1927 in Marion, Alabama, Coretta Scott spent her young years on the farm of her parents, Obie Leonard Scott and Bernice McMurray Scott. Coretta's maternal grandfather was part American Indian with straight black hair and fair features, much like those of Coretta herself. Her paternal grandfather, Jeff Scott, a farmer, became a prominent figure in the rural black community, especially in church affairs.

Among the most successful black figures in Marion, Obie Scott was the first man in the town to own a truck, which he used for a lumber hauling business. He maintained his small farm, learned the barbering trade, and tirelessly pressed to achieve whatever independence was possible under the racial conditions that surrounded him.

Overcoming long odds, Obie and Bernice Scott managed to acquire enough money to be able to encourage their children to fight for a college education, which had been impossible for the two of them.

Along with the rest of her family, including her sister Edythe and brother Obie, Jr., Coretta was always fearful of possible violence against her father. Retribution against blacks who challenged white supremacy in the South was commonplace. Never one to grovel at the feet of whites, Obie Scott stood his ground, often incurring racial insults and threats. One of Coretta's great-uncles was lynched.

"In 1942, our family home burned down Thanksgiving weekend, and we suspected arson," Coretta later remembered. "But in the racial and political climate of the 1940's, we had no recourse. Daddy simply kept working, eventually built us a new house, and even saved up enough money to buy a sawmill. When he refused to sell his mill to a White man, he was threatened; two weeks later Daddy found his sawmill burned to a pile of ashes. Again, there was nothing for him to do but to go back to work hauling lumber for other people."[7]

After graduating from Lincoln High School, a private black institution with an integrated faculty, Coretta followed her sister into Antioch College in Yellow Springs, Ohio, a liberal arts school that traced it roots to 1853. Its first president, Horace Mann, a champion of public schools in the United States, was attracted to Antioch by the decision of its trustees that the school become the first institution of higher learning in the nation to admit women as degree candidates on the same footing as men. Through the years, Antioch developed a reputation as a center for artistic and cultural activity and high academic achievement.

Majoring in both education and music, she was deeply disappointed to find out that she would not be able to teach in a public school because of her race. She soon became involved with a number of civil rights groups, including the Antioch chapter of the NAACP, as well as the Young Progressives, and she attended the Progressive Party convention in 1948 as a student delegate. She received her B.A. in music and elementary education from Antioch in 1949.

Because of her extraordinary musical talent, her teachers suggested she further her education at a music conservatory. In 1951, with the help of a grant from the Jessie Smith Noyes Foundation, she enrolled at Boston's New England Conservatory of Music, eventually earning a Mus.B. in voice.

It was through a mutual friend, Mary Powell, that Martin met Coretta. At first, Coretta was reluctant to meet the young theology student. "The moment Mary told me the young man was a minister, I lost interest, for I began to think of the stereotypes of ministers I had known—fundamentalists in their thinking, very narrow, and overly pious."[8] In addition, as a first-year student at the conservatory, Coretta saw an education and a career in music in her immediate future; she did not see ahead a relationship with a preacher.

But Mary Powell persisted, telling Coretta about the King family and the Twelfth Baptist Church in Roxbury where Martin sometimes preached. She decided to see him. After their first phone conversation, Martin told her, "I'm coming from Boston University. I usually make it in 10 minutes, but tomorrow, I'll make it in 7." They agreed to meet at Sharaf's restaurant on Massachusetts Avenue.[9]

"This young man became increasingly better-looking as he talked, so strongly and convincingly," she said later. "In our discussion I must have made some reasonably intelligent comments, for he said, 'Oh, I see you know more about some other things besides music.'"[10]

"This guy had a sensitivity, intelligence and seriousness of purpose that you didn't find in other young men his age," Coretta wrote. "He was a good dancer too. He had a wonderful sense of humor and a way of making everyone he came into contact with feel very special, including me."[11]

King was immediately taken by her charm, personality, and striking looks. Early on, his thoughts turned toward marriage. Her took her to a party. When other young women fawned over him, he maintained a calm, assured presence, carefully attentive to her. He took her to Boston Symphony Hall to hear the eminent pianist Artur Rubinstein. They went ice-skating and talked philosophy. They went to the shore, bought clams, and walked along the ocean.

He talked about preaching and about the fact that his father had hoped he would marry a girl King knew in Atlanta and would settle down at Ebenezer to preach with him. And then he told her that he had no intention of marrying the girl in Atlanta. They talked about their ideas of marriage. King strongly believed that the wife should care for the children at home and not hand off that responsibility to others. But he emphasized that the last thing he sought in a wife was someone with no independence and ideas of her own. He wanted someone with whom he could share dreams and tackle social issues, and someone who would be not only a lover but also a partner. Finally, he asked her to be his wife.

Although she had reservations over the differences in their backgrounds and although her own aspirations for a career in music would be jeopardized by a marriage with King, she accepted the proposal from the young minister.

The two were married on the lawn of the Scott family home on June 18, 1953, by Martin Luther King Sr. Edythe Bagley, Mrs. King's sister, served as maid of honor, and the Reverend A. D. King, Martin Luther King, Jr.'s brother, as the best man.

They spent their first night of marriage in the home of a Scott family friend who was an undertaker. Later, King would joke, "Do you know we spent our honeymoon at a funeral parlor?"[12]

"If Martin hadn't come to Boston, he would have never met her," said John Cartwright. "If he hadn't met someone of her character, of her intelligence, he might never have led the life he did."[13]

They would have four children: Yolanda Denise, born November 17, 1955 in Montgomery, Alabama; Martin Luther III, born October 23,

1957 in Montgomery; Dexter Scott, born January 30, 1961 in Atlanta, Georgia; and Bernice Albertine, born March 28, 1963 in Atlanta.

DEXTER AVENUE BAPTIST CHURCH

King and his young wife moved into a four-room apartment and continued their studies. As he neared the end of his class requirements and began to write his doctoral dissertation, he began seriously to consider what type of employment he might first accept to begin his career. Although some of his advisors encouraged him to seek an academic or administrative appointment in a college or university, King decided to follow his ultimate career path toward the ministry.

As King finished his work at Boston University, Dexter Avenue Baptist Church in Montgomery, Alabama was without a pastor. Its latest, Vernon Johns, had been a man on a mission to turn Dexter into an activist church, a congregation that would not turn the other cheek to racism and second-class citizenship, an institution that would spark a social reform movement against segregation and discrimination. Flamboyant and eccentric, Johns began to antagonize many members of his flock with such sermons as "It's Safe to Murder Negroes in Montgomery" and "Segregation after Death."

For much of the black community of Montgomery, Alabama, Dexter Avenue Baptist Church held a kind of defiant symbolism. The church had stood for over a century amidst a number of impressive buildings near the center of town, including the Alabama State Capitol. It was here at the Capitol in January 1861 that Jefferson Davis of Mississippi had taken his oath as president of the Confederate States of America. It was here that the first Confederate flag waved. This was, indeed, "The Cradle of the Confederacy."

The red brick church across from the Capitol traced its lineage to a hall on Market Place where a group of black citizens first gathered soon after the Civil War to form the congregation. The hall had once been the site of a slave pen, where thousands of blacks over the years had been bought and sold. In 1889, worshippers first gathered in the new sanctuary.

Although most members of the church likely agreed with the general beliefs espoused by Johns, they began to chafe under his increasingly vehement demands that they join a social revolution. He began to sell produce at church functions to encourage parishioners to boycott white-owned businesses. He led a number of black passengers off a bus in Montgomery to demonstrate the evils of segregated seating. A growing number of the congregation came to believe that Johns was an embarrassment to the church. In September 1952, Vernon Johns's stormy leadership of Dexter ended. The church looked for new, less raucous leadership.

Dexter had tended to go through ministers quickly. Robert D. Nesbitt, who had headed several pulpit committees to seek out replacements, was again on the job after the departure of Johns.

While visiting Atlanta on business, Nesbitt mentioned to a friend the vacancy at Dexter. The friend had an immediate suggestion—young King, son of Martin Luther King, Sr., pastor of Ebenezer Baptist Church, two blocks away. Could this new search be as simple as this? Nesbitt arranged to visit King, who was on holiday from school. He found the young preacher in the dinning room finishing some pork chops. Nesbitt's conversation with King led to an invitation to preach.

In the spring of 1954, King drove to Montgomery to preach. Dexter was not as large as Ebenezer, seating around 400 people. In Ebenezer, King had preached to congregations of over 700. Although small, Dexter attracted a relatively affluent congregation within the black community. Many of its members had college degrees, and many were successful business leaders, physicians, and teachers. Lower-class blacks in Montgomery referred to it as the "big people's church." King was impressed with the church and its people.

They were also impressed with him. In the summer, King received an offer to become Dexter's twentieth pastor.

"I think he liked what he saw, and we liked what we saw," said Nesbitt. "However, there were one or two old-timers who said, 'That little boy can't preach to us.'" Looking back, Nesbitt said, "I firmly believe I was in the right place at the right time and God had a purpose for this man."[14] Although he considered other offers from churches to be their pastor and three offers for administrative and teaching positions at colleges, King, after preaching twice at Dexter, accepted the church's call.

Coretta King later wrote: "After graduating from the conservatory I had gone to stay with Mamma and Daddy King in Atlanta while Martin remained in Boston to finish his dissertation. That July weekend, on his trip to Montgomery, he took me with him to meet his new congregation. Dexter was a fine, solid, Victorian brick church, standing on Montgomery's handsome public square.... The 'official' white southern square was an odd place for a Negro Church, but Dexter had been built in Reconstruction days, when Negroes were enjoying their brief freedom after the Civil War. At that time blacks owned various properties in downtown Montgomery, but they were all eventually pushed out."[15]

Because he had not yet completed his doctoral dissertation, King was given the pastorate at Dexter on the condition that he would not be required to begin full-time duties until September 1, 1954. For the next four months, he traveled by plane between Boston and Montgomery. He would be awarded his Ph.D. in June 1955.

King and his wife moved into the parsonage on September 1, 1954, and King's installation service was held at the church two months later. King's father traveled from Atlanta to preach the sermon and brought with him around 100 family members and friends.

Shortly after he began his pastorate, King changed the church's handling of its finances and established a building fund and renovation program. More revealing of his larger agenda, he proposed a number of recommendations that revealed his passion for social change. Every member of Dexter, King said, should become a registered voter. In addition, they should join the NAACP. He organized a social and political action committee to encourage church members to become politically active and informed of important social and economic issues of the day.

"After I lived in Montgomery about a year," King wrote, "I became the proud father of a little daughter-Yolanda Denise. 'Yoki' was a big little girl-she weighed nine pounds and eleven ounces. She kept her father quite busy walking the floor."[16]

NOTES

1. *Boston Globe*, April 23, 1965.

2. Cara Feinberg, "When Martin Met Coretta: One Studied at BU; Another at the Conservatory: Both Strolled the same Mass. Ave. Blocks," *Boston Globe*, January 19, 2003.

3. Feinberg.

4. Clayborne Carson, ed., *The Autobiography of Martin Luther King, Jr.* (New York: Warner Books, 1998), p. 32.

5. Stephen B. Oates, *Let the Trumpet Sound: The Life of Martin Luther King, Jr.* (New York: New American Library, 1982), p. 40.

6. Feinberg.

7. Corretta Scott King, as told to Joy Duckett Cain, "Family on the Front Line," *Essence*, December 1999, p. 102.

8. Coretta Scott King, *My Life with Martin Luther King, Jr.* (New York: Holt, Rinehart and Winston, 1969), p. 52.

9. Cara Feinberg, "For Coretta, Finding Her Direction," *Boston Globe*, January 19, 2003, p. 11.

10. King, *My Life Wwith Martin Luther King, Jr.*, pp. 54–55.

11. King, "Family on the Front Line," p. 102.

12. Oates, p. 44.

13. Feinberg, "For Coretta, Finding Her Direction," p. 11.

14. Gayle White, "In King's Shadow: Montgomery's Dexter Avenue Baptist Church Struggles to Regain a Lost Dynamism and Find its Place in the '90s," *The Atlanta Journal-Constitution*, February 25, 1996.

15. King, *My Life with Martin Luther King*, pp. 98–99.

16. Carson, p. 49.

Chapter 4

MONTGOMERY AND THE
ROAD TO CIVIL RIGHTS

From his earliest days as pastor of Dexter, King had managed thoroughly to charm the congregation, fast becoming a figure in whom they could trust and to whom they could bare their souls. For King himself, his immersion in this deep South black church, filled with its traditions and dignity, aroused his emotions. The call-and-response dialogue of the preacher with his followers, so long a fixture in their African ancestry, came naturally to King.

At Dexter he could lose himself in the spirit and energy of a people seeking power against the systems and fates that had so long held them down. "And I tell you *[tell it doctor]* that any religion that professes to be concerned with the souls of men *[well awright]* and is not concerned with the slums that damn them *[amen, brother]* and the social conditions that cripple them *[oh, yes]* is a dry-as-dust religion *[well]*. Religion deals with both heaven and earth *[yes]*, time and eternity *[uhhuh]*, seeking not only to integrate man with God *[clapping, clapping!]* but man with man."[1]

He was so young, yet so dynamic, that many older parishioners did not quite know what to make of him. Word of the young preacher's talent spread quickly throughout black communities. From as far away as Pennsylvania, invitations to preach reached his desk. In December 1954, Daddy King wrote to his son, "Every way I turn people are congratulating me for you. You see young man you are becoming very popular.... Persons like yourself are the ones the devil turns loose all his forces to destroy."[2]

As King's visibility increased among the black citizens of Montgomery, so did his involvement in activities aimed at the unconscionable segregation under which blacks in the South had to live. If the devil would turn his forces loose on the young preacher, as his father suggested, he did not seem to be one who would back down.

In Montgomery, 50,000 black citizens lived with 70,000 white citizens in an uncomfortable truce controlled by laws, force, and a culture of domination. Almost all of Montgomery's black citizens, in almost all of their conditions of life, from housing to schooling, existed in a kind of second-world status, catering to the whims and comforts of their white counterparts. Only 2,000 blacks in the city could vote. All lived in a condition of enforced inferiority, with "whites only" signs only one reminder every day of their social condition.

King was as angry and defiant about the racial condition as Vernon Johns had been, and the young preacher began, in his own determined way, to lead his church toward social protest. Dexter was soon contributing more to the NAACP than any other black church in the city. King was elected to the executive committee of the Montgomery chapter of the NAACP and became a member of the Alabama Council on Human Relations.

THE FIRE OF E. D. NIXON

At an NAACP meeting at the Metropolitan Methodist Church in August 1955, King delivered a typically ringing speech about the need for social action. In the audience was a long-time social activist named Edgar Nixon.

When he was in his twenties, Nixon had been a Pullman porter. In 1925 Labor leader A. Philip Randolph began to organize a union of black Pullman porters and Nixon was an immediate convert. When he heard Randolph speak, he said later, it was if a great light had shone. "Before that time, I figured that a Negro would be kicked around and accept whatever the white man did. I never knew the Negro had a right to enjoy freedom like everyone else. When Randolph stood there and talked that day, it made a different man of me. From that day on, I was determined that I was gonna fight for freedom until I was able to get some of it myself."[3]

By 1938, Nixon had founded the Montgomery, Alabama Division of the union and served as its president for 25 years. In the 1930s, Nixon also joined Myles Horton of Tennessee's Highlander Folk School in an attempt to organize Alabama's cucumber pickers in a union. Nixon became such a central figure among Montgomery's black community that black citizens arrested in the city often called Nixon if they had no one to bail them out of jail. Vernon Johns, King's predecessor at Dexter, often accompanied Nixon on some of these emergency runs, many very late at night.

Tall, raspy-voiced, his lack of a formal education offset by an angry militancy, Edgar Nixon was on a mission. He was looking for the right incident and the right circumstances to attempt to challenge the city law that segregated whites from blacks in the seats of city buses. He was looking for an opportunity for Montgomery to make its own strike for his fellow blacks against a world of injustice, to make its own contribution to an already long overdue struggle for civil rights.

A LONG ROAD TOWARD JUSTICE

In 1898, the Supreme Court's *Plessy v. Ferguson* decision had legitimized the practice of railroads providing "separate but equal" accommodations for black and white citizens. The case involved Homer Plessy, a black man who, defying the law, sat in the white section of a railroad car. Initially fined $25, Plessy contested the decision all the way to the Supreme Court. The high court upheld the state's separate but equal doctrine. It was this decision against which reformers would battle long into the twentieth century.

Plessy v. Ferguson led to more than just separate railroad cars. Schools, restaurants, courthouses, bathrooms, and even drinking fountains were also segregated. "Whites Only" signs became common. The law influenced most kinds of interactions between blacks and whites. The decision in 1898 exemplified the race hatred plaguing the country, a time that saw over 1,000 lynchings in the 1890s and a series of race riots after the turn of the century.

In 1948, the politics of race raised its fierce and ominous form, sparked by two significant developments on the civil rights road. The first was President Harry S Truman's decision to integrate the army. Although blacks had served in the armed forces since the American Revolution, they were, as in other aspects of society, segregated, assigned to all-black, mostly noncombat units. Living in separate barracks, they ate in separate dining halls. Spurred by the performance of black troops in World War II, by the urging of civil rights groups, and by a report issued by a presidential Committee on Civil Rights, Truman issued an executive order. It guaranteed equal treatment for all persons in the armed services regardless of race, color, or national origin.

Also in 1948, a young mayor of Minneapolis, Minnesota, Hubert Humphrey, led liberals in a successful fight at the Democratic Party convention to put a strong civil rights plank in the party platform.

Feeling angered and betrayed by the direction of the party, a number of southern delegates rebelled, formed a separate party whose message was simply to denounce race intermingling, called themselves "Dixiecrats," and carried four southern states in the 1948 election.

In postwar America, despite the fact that President Truman had integrated military service, very little had changed for the black communities across America, especially in the South. Harry Ashmore, former editor of the *Arkansas Gazette*, said, "World War II had changed that whole pattern of people's thinking, and I used to say that we're coming to the point—and you could see it coming—where whites were not willing to accept blacks on a basis of equality, and blacks were no longer willing to accept anything else. So there was a collision coming."[4]

In 1954, the same year that young Martin Luther King, Jr. preached his first sermon at Dexter, the United States Supreme Court, in the decision *Brown v. Board of Education* finally struck down the doctrine of "separate but equal," enunciated in the *Plessy v. Fergusen* case. Black community leaders in Topeka, Kansas, aided by the local chapter of the NAACP, brought suit against the Board of Education of Topeka Schools, arguing that their children were being denied equal education. The court, in a unanimous decision, stated that the "separate but equal" clause was unconstitutional because it violated the children's 14th amendment rights by separating them solely on the classification of the color of their skin. In delivering the court's opinion, Chief Justice Earl Warren declared, "We conclude that in the field of education the doctrine of 'separate but equal' has no place. Separate educational facilities are inherently unequal."[5]

Although the court's decision did not abolish segregation in other public areas, such as restaurants and restrooms, it did, however, declare the permissive or mandatory segregation that existed in 21 states unconstitutional. It was a giant step toward desegregation. It was now Montgomery, Alabama's, turn.

ROSA PARKS AND THE MONTGOMERY BUS BOYCOTT

In Montgomery, as in cities across the South, blacks lived through indignities large and small. Especially noxious, because they affected a large number of blacks every day of their lives, were the rules under which they could ride the city buses.

Approximately 75 percent of bus riders in Montgomery were black; all of the bus drivers were white. The drivers routinely addressed their clientele with racial epithets. In order to ride the bus, a black person would have to walk up the front steps, pay the fare, back out of the bus, walk to the rear, and enter through the back door. Often, blacks who had already paid their fares watched as the buses pulled away without them. Once inside, a black passenger could not sit in any of the first four rows. A sign saying "Whites Only" made that rule perfectly clear. If all of the front whites only seats were taken, a white passenger could then choose any other seat on the bus. If that white passenger sat next to a black individual, the black person was required to stand up. City regulations did not allow whites and blacks to sit next to each other on buses. If black passengers had filled up the back of the buses and the front four rows were empty, blacks could still not sit in any of those seats.

In December 1955, shortly over a year since King had been pastor at Dexter, a black woman named Rosa Parks, a seamstress for the Montgomery Fair department store at Court Square in the heart of downtown, crossed a significant dividing line and the civil rights movement never looked back. Born in Tuskegee, Alabama in 1913, she grew up in Montgomery and was educated at Alabama State College. In 1932 she married Raymond Parks, a barber at the Atlas Barber Shop and an active member of the NAACP.

In 1943, Parks was hired as secretary of the local chapter of the NAACP, and by the late 1940s, she was named secretary of the Alabama State Conference of NAACP branches. In 1954, she reorganized the NAACP Youth Council, for which she served as adult advisor.

Rosa Parks knew well the Montgomery, Alabama law requiring blacks to surrender their seats on public buses if segregated white sections were full. She was also convinced that any challenge to the law should be done with nonviolence, dignity, and determination.

On Thursday, December 1, 1955, she boarded the Cleveland Avenue bus, deposited her 10¢ fare, backed out of the bus, entered through the rear door, and took a seat in the first row of the "colored" section in the back, along with three other individuals. A few stops later, the front rows were filled with whites, and one white man was left standing. According to law, blacks and whites could not occupy the same row, so the bus driver asked the blacks seated in the first "colored" section to move. Three complied, but Parks refused. The driver notified the police, who arrested Parks for violating city and state ordinances. She was released on $100 bond.

In Parks's arrest, black leaders, led by Nixon, saw a perfect opportunity to challenge the city's segregated bus system. Nixon and others, especially Jo Ann Robinson, a professor of English at Alabama State College and long-time civil rights worker, quickly began to mobilize forces. King later wrote of Robinson: "Apparently indefatigable, she, perhaps more than any other person, was active on every level of the protest."[6]

Nixon was convinced that King, a relative newcomer but powerful orator, would be the most effective leader of a boycott of Montgomery's city buses. Nixon and others contacted King and asked if he would lead a meeting in the basement of Dexter. Nixon had more in mind than merely using Dexter as a meeting place. He wanted to put King in a position that would make it impossible for him to resist a call for leadership.

At first, King wanted time to think it over. Nixon then turned to Ralph Abernathy, a 29-year-old pastor of Montgomery's First Baptist Church, the second oldest black church in the city. King and Abernathy had already become close friends and Abernathy was able to persuade King to host the meeting. At the meeting, Nixon, Abernathy, and the others persuaded King to become involved with the boycott. By the next morning, King was helping to mimeograph leaflets announcing a boycott by blacks of Montgomery's city buses to begin on Monday, December 5, the day of the scheduled trial of Rosa Parks.

On Sunday, King preached a sermon the congregation might have expected from his predecessor, Vernon Johns. This was not an abstract sermon about biblical truths but a call for social protest. He asked the congregation not to ride the city buses.

On Monday morning, December 5, 1955, King got up before dawn, made a cup of coffee, and walked to the front window of his house. He and Coretta watched with amazement as several buses, their interiors lit in early morning darkness, passed by his home carrying no passengers. King got dressed, rushed to his car, picked up Ralph Abernathy, and drove around areas of Montgomery's black community. The sight was eerie. Except for a few whites and only a scant number of blacks, the buses rolled by with almost no one on them. No clusters of blacks waited at bus stops. The black citizens of Montgomery had responded beyond King's wildest hopes. The boycott was underway.

Flushed with joy at the first day's success, Nixon, Jo Ann Robinson, and others quickly arranged a meeting of the city's ministers that night at Holt Street Baptist Church to discuss the possibility of extending the boycott to a long-term campaign. It was during this meeting that the Montgomery Improvement Association was formed and that Nixon and the others put forward King's nomination as president. He accepted.

"The action had caught me unawares," King later wrote. "It had happened so quickly I did not even have time to think it through. It is probable that if I had, I would have declined the nomination."[7]

Nearly bewildered by this sudden turn in his life, King nevertheless, responded to the large crowd jammed into a local church with an astonishing sense of purpose. He began slowly, with each word distinct and firm: "We are here this evening—for serious business." They waited with hushed expectation. "We are here in a general sense, because first and foremost—we are American citizens—and we are determined to apply our citizenship—to the fullness of its means."[8]

With each rise and fall of inflection, with each new powerful phrase, the crowd became a congregation, and calls in unison of "Amen" and "Yes, sir" began to pour out from the audience. "And we are determined here in Montgomery," he declared, using biblical lines from the Book of Amos, "to work and fight until justice runs down like water, and righteousness like a mighty stream." The crowd roared. They were with him and with the cause.[9]

Nixon was asked later about his role in the selection of King to lead the boycott. "I had to be sure," he said, "that I had somebody I could win with."[10]

In the coming days, King appealed to the city's black citizens for nonviolent responses to any aggressive assaults made by whites. King and the other leaders distributed pamphlets that suggested, "If cursed, do not curse back. If pushed, do not push back. If struck, do not strike back, but evidence … goodwill at all times." If another person suffers an attack, they said, "do not rise to go to his defense, but pray for the oppressor and use moral and spiritual force to carry on the struggle for justice."[11]

In taking up this enormous responsibility, extremely dangerous and daunting, King later said that his religious conviction took hold as never before. "And I discovered then that religion had to become real to me," he said, "and I had to know God for myself … and I prayed out loud that night. I said, 'Lord, I'm down here trying to do what's right. I think the cause that we represent is right. But Lord, I must confess that I'm weak now. I'm faltering. I'm losing my courage. And I can't let the people see me like this because if they see me weak and losing my courage they will begin to get weak.' And it seemed at that moment that I could hear an inner voice saying to me, 'Martin Luther, stand up for righteousness. Stand up for justice. Stand up for truth. And I will be with you, even until the end of the world. …' Almost at once my fears began to go. My uncertainty disappeared."[12]

When the boycott began, no one expected it to last for very long. On Thursday, December 8, the fourth day, King and black leaders met with representatives of the bus company, along with city commissioners, to present a moderate desegregation plan. They hoped their demands would be accepted and that the boycott would come to an end.

But King's diplomatic efforts met with cold defiance from city and bus company leaders. Not only did the bus company reject the plan, it announced that any cab driver charging less than the 45-cent minimum fare would be prosecuted. Since the boycott began, the black cab services had been charging blacks only 10 cents to ride, the same as the bus fare, but this service would be no more. The battle was joined.

Suddenly the boycotters were faced with the prospect of having thousands of blacks with no way to get to work, and with no end to the boycott in sight. Undeterred, they organized a "private taxi" plan, under which blacks who owned cars picked up and dropped off individuals who needed rides at designated points. Rufus Lewis, an undertaker at the Ross-Clayton Funeral Home, had access to a fleet of funeral cars and became the boycott's transportation chief. Although elaborate, the transportation plan worked so well that some members of the White Citizens Council likened it to a military drill.

King had believed that if they could get 60 percent cooperation the protest would be a success. Later, as he watched empty buses continue to roll through Montgomery's black communities, he knew the magnitude of the protest. He later wrote, "A miracle had taken place. The once dormant and quiescent Negro community was now fully awake."[13]

From that first Monday morning in early December, the boycott took rigid hold. In the cold of winter, even on bitter rainy days, many blacks—maids and charwomen, janitors and hod carriers—trudged the streets, refusing to get on Montgomery's buses. It was as if the boycott had unleashed the frustrations and feelings of powerlessness that had so long gripped these people. This was their chance to come together and they took it. One man rode a mule to work. One elderly grandmother commented, "It used to be my soul was tired and my feet rested; now my feet's tired, but my soul is rested."[14]

As tensions in the city grew with each day, black citizens did not back down. One woman named Georgia Gilmore later remembered, "I only got into real trouble one time. A white man had a grocery around the corner. Now I sent the child down there to get a loaf and he brought home a stale loaf. So I went on back up there myself and he started cussing me. I guess the pressure of the boycott and all had got to him. I guess it got to me. I grabbed him. Right in his own store. I had him down on the floor. I had him in a headlock. I took a real chance, but nothing ever happened to me. Afterward, I went up and talked to my priest. He said, 'Georgia, you got to control your temper.' Just like Reverend King says, 'Just don't pay 'em any attention and they'll go away.' Course, that time I paid 'im a little attention."[15]

As leader of the new Montgomery Improvement Association and the boycott, King became the focus of white hatred. On the afternoon of January 26,1956, as he was helping drive black citizens to their jobs, King was pulled over by police on motorcycles. They claimed he had exceeded the 25 miles per hour limit. Instead of simply issuing him a ticket, they pulled him out of the car, frisked him, hustled him into a squad car that seemed to come out of nowhere, and drove him to a police station in a northern section of Montgomery far from his home.

While alone in a jail cell for the first time, the young minister who had been catapulted into the center of a smoldering moment in the history of the South wondered whether the end had already come. Would he be spirited out of jail and taken to some isolated woods to be strung up, to suffer the same fate as so many other blacks in the past who had challenged white authority?

Word of King's arrest swiftly reverberated around the black community, and when reporters found the location of the jail a massive crowd began to assemble outside. The police, fearful of repercussions, released the prisoner.

Four days later, on January 30, 1956, the violence that King knew he would have to face hit very close to home. Fearful that thugs opposed to the boycott might attack his wife and child, King arranged to have fellow church members stay with them while he was working at night. On an evening when King was with Abernathy and others at a meeting, church member Mary Lucy Williams stayed in the house with Coretta and the baby. Suddenly, about 9:30, a loud thud and then a thunderous blast hit the King home, followed by heavy smoke, and the sounds of shattering glass. Fortunately the three inside scrambled to the back, shaken but unhurt by the bomb.

Quickly, neighbors gathered at the house to see whether there had been injuries. The police were called and friends contacted King, who rushed home. As word of the bombing circulated through the streets of Montgomery, the crowd swelled in size, many calling for retribution, some carrying guns and knives. The house filled with friends, church members, neighbors, and white reporters. Montgomery's mayor and police commissioner feared the worst.

When King arrived he made certain that Coretta and Yoki were not injured and then he faced the large crowd in front of the house. Coretta later remembered: "At that point Martin walked out on the porch. In some ways it was the most important hour of his life. His own home had just been bombed, his wife and baby could have been killed; this was the first deep test of his Christian principles and his theories of nonviolence. Standing there, very grave and calm, he dominated those furious people." He held up his hand, Mrs. King remembered, and asked the crowd to disperse, to put down any weapons. "We cannot solve this problem through retaliatory violence," he said. "We must meet violence with nonviolence. Remember the words of Jesus: 'He who lives by the sword will perish by the sword.' We must love our white brothers, no matter what they do to us. We must make them know that we love them. Jesus still cries out across the centuries, 'Love your enemies.' This is what we must live by. We must meet hate with love."[16]

Slowly, uncertainly, the crowd backed away. A white policeman in the middle of the crowd told a fellow officer that if it had not been for the preacher, the two of them might have been killed.

King and his family spent the night in the home of a member of his congregation. In the early morning hours, King's father, fresh from driving to Montgomery from Atlanta, managed to find the whereabouts of his son. At about 4:00 in the morning, the two argued over the immediate future. The father wanted the son to leave Montgomery and return with him to Atlanta. The situation had so spiraled out of control, was so volatile, that tragedy was becoming inevitable. The son refused to leave. The moral stakes were too great, he responded. To abandon Montgomery at this time would be to forfeit all he believed and would do irreparable damage to the civil rights cause. He would stay.

In the coming days, King's assuring presence and his flowing rhetoric to overflow crowds at mass meetings sustained the boycott. Suddenly, this young new minister in a major city relatively unknown to him was aggressively taking charge, organizing carpools to serve boycotters, planning strategy with other black leaders, helping the boycott gain momentum, and calming an anxious citizenry.

A few days later, the home of E. D. Nixon was bombed with his wife, Arlet, inside. Like Coretta King, Arlet Nixon was not hurt in the bombing. The Nixons also refused to be intimidated. As the boycott progressed, Nixon made a number of trips to northern cities raising money from civil rights supporters to help pay the expenses of boycotters. He came back from those trips with nearly $100,000.

The white power structure of Montgomery tried in every way to fend off what it regarded correctly as nothing less than an insult to authority and a challenge to a way of life. Montgomery Mayor W. A. "Tacky" Gayle declared, "The white people are firm in their convictions that they do not care whether the Negroes ever ride a city bus again if it means that the social fabric of our community is to be destroyed."[17]

The Christmas season of 1956 was unlike any that the city of Montgomery had ever experienced. In addition to the usual sermons about peace on earth and the Christian ideals of love and brotherhood, ministers now dealt with the implications to their faiths of the race question. As shoppers, white and black, walked the streets of the city looking for gifts, they heard on some streetcorners, along with Salvation Army bells, the sounds of a protest song:

Ain't gonna ride them buses no more

Ain't gonna ride them buses no more....[18]

At first, whites tried to divide the black community. In late January the City Commission met with three black ministers who were not directly involved with the boycott and proposed an arrangement, which was not appreciably different than the system already in place. The intimidated ministers gave their verbal approval to the so-called compromise and newspapers soon got word from the city negotiators that the boycott was over.

To counteract any rumors or false stories in the press from deceiving the black community, King and the Montgomery Improvement Association responded quickly. Members of the organization contacted black ministers and fanned out across the black neighborhoods, in restaurants, bars, and stores to spread the word that any news that the boycott was over was merely a white plot to disrupt the protest. Later, the black ministers who had been lured into accepting the so-called compromise told King they had been misled. The buses remained empty of black passengers on Monday morning.

White citizens' groups next sought action in the courts. On February 21, 1956, 89 blacks were indicted under an old law prohibiting boycotts. King was the first defendant to be tried. As a growing press contingent from around the country began to spread the news of the boycott, King was ordered to pay $500 plus $500 in court costs or spend 386 days in the state penitentiary. King and his supporters managed to pay the fines. In addition, the white power structure had merely once again given King greater visibility and a platform to spell out what nonviolent protest was all about. "If we are trampled every day," he said to the boycotters, "don't ever let anyone pull you down so low as to hate them. We must use the weapon of love, we must have compassion and understanding for those who hate us."[19]

Led by King and a growing number of supporters, the protesters held a succession of meetings in various secret locations, including the rooftop of the Ben Moore Hotel, one of the premier black hotels of the South. They planned strategy, kept up the momentum, and refused to back down, despite continuing harassment and violence. Reverend Abernathy's church took the brunt of several explosions and his home was bombed as well. A bomb explosion rocked the home of a Lutheran minister, reducing the structure to a pile of boards and splinters. Other black churches were hit with varying degrees of destruction. The threats on King's life escalated and he began to see a kind of inevitability to later injury or death. But this experience changed his life and the lives of so many others involved. They were now all part of a movement that seemed much larger than their own individual lives.

Legally, the boycott leaders were armed with the Supreme Court's decision in the *Brown v. Board of Education* case, now less than two years old. Because the Brown case affirmed that the "separate but equal" doctrine did not apply to public schools, logic seemed to indicate that if a similar case regarding public buses could reach the court, the ruling might be similar. Black leaders, therefore, looked forward to a legal challenge. They filed suit in a federal court.

When a three-judge panel ruled in June that Montgomery's bus segregation was unconstitutional, the city quickly appealed the decision, hoping to tie the issue up the court system for years to come. Their hopes were shattered. The U.S. Supreme Court, on November 13, 1956, upheld the federal court's ruling, declaring segregation on buses unconstitutional. The Montgomery bus boycott was officially over.

Black people had walked and hitched rides and created a virtual bus system of their own in bringing the bus company to its knees. The boycott lasted 381 days and was honored by virtually 100 percent of Montgomery's black riders. Montgomery City Lines lost between 30,000 and 40,000 bus fares each day during the boycott. Nevertheless, the company reluctantly desegregated its buses only after the Supreme Court ruling.

As blacks returned to the buses on December 21, 1956, agitators were not finished. Snipers shot at buses at night, forcing the city to suspend bus hours after 5:00 P.M. One group decided to try to start a whites-only bus service, an effort soon aborted. In addition, bombers were still attempting to terrorize. They hit the homes of two of the boycott leaders, several churches, a service station, and a taxicab stand.

The Ku Klux Klan (KKK), the aging but still determined hate group, also continued to try to scare the blacks, but, according to King, "it seemed to have lost its spell." "[O]ne cold night a small Negro boy was seen warming his hands at a burning cross," King recalled.[20]

Martin Luther King's leadership of the Montgomery bus boycott was a call to action, a catalyst that would drive the civil rights movement for many years. National attention was now focused on the dynamic King.

And for much of Montgomery's black population, the victory in the bus boycott was a strong affirmation of self-worth. As one black janitor said, "We got our heads up now and we won't ever bow down again—no, sir—except before God."[21]

NOTES

1. Stephen B. Oates, *Let the Trumpet Sound: The Life of Martin Luther King, Jr.* (New York: Mentor, 1982), p. 53. Emphasis in original.

2. Oates, pp. 53–54.

3. Billy Bowles, "E. D. Nixon Guided Generation toward Civil Rights Movement," *Houston Chronicle*, March 8, 1987.

4. "Will the Circle be Unbroken? Episode 12: Nine for Justice," http://unbrokencircle.org/focus_week06.htm.

5. "The Promise and the Legacy: Fifty Years After Brown v. Board of Education," http://k12.brown.edu/brownvboard/.

6. Martin Luther King, Jr., *Stride Toward Freedom* (New York: Harper and Row, 1958), p. 78.

7. Bowles.

8. Taylor Branch, *Parting the Waters: America in the King Years 1954–63* (New York: Touchstone, 1988), p. 140.

9. Branch, p. 141.

10. Juan Williams, *Eyes on the Prize: America's Civil Rights Years, 1954–1965* (New York: Viking Penguin, 1987), pp. 62–63.

11. "Integrated Bus Suggestions," *Mighty Times: The Legacy of Rosa Parks*, Teaching Tolerance, A Project of the Southern Poverty Law Center: 2002, p. 24.

12. David Garrow, *Bearing the Cross: Martin Luther King, Jr. and the Southern Christian Leadership Conference* (New York: William Morrow, 1986), p. 58.

13. Williams, p. 69.

14. Coretta Scott King, *My Life with Martin Luther King, Jr.* (New York: Holt Rinehart and Winston, 1969), p. 21.

15. Paul Hendrickson, "Montgomery: The Supporting Actors in the Historic Bus Boycott," *Washington Post*, July 24, 1989.

16. Coretta Scott King, pp. 128–30.

17. Marshall Frady, *Martin Luther King, Jr.* (New York: Viking, Penguin, 2000), p. 37.

18. Oates, p. 81.

19. Frady, p. 40.

20. Martin Luther King, Jr., p.175.

21. Oates, p. 109.

Chapter 5

A GROWING MOVEMENT

THE SOUTHERN CHRISTIAN LEADERSHIP CONFERENCE

On January 10, 1957, soon after Montgomery's black citizens had begun to ride buses without the baggage of indignity and humiliation, King was in Atlanta. At Ebenezer, he met with a number of black leaders to lay out plans to create an organization that would maintain the gathering momentum for change that the bus boycott had unleashed.

The Supreme Court decision had fueled the passion and determination of King and his followers, and they were not about to rest on their laurels, not about to let go of this opportunity to make a difference across the South. Unlike the NAACP, an organization that concentrated most of its efforts on legal challenges, voter registration drives, and other constitutional efforts, this would be a grass-roots protest movement, action oriented, using the tactics of nonviolent confrontation that had been ultimately so successful in Montgomery.

As King and the others gathered in Atlanta, they received word that violence had again broken out in Montgomery. Six bombs had exploded at parsonages and churches in the early morning of January 10, 1957. King and Abernathy flew back to Montgomery.

As they toured the sights where the bombs had exploded, they saw ominous crowds of blacks milling around talking about retaliation. One old man told King, "When they bomb the house of the Lord, we are dealing with crazy people."[1]

Weary of the extreme tension and ominous foreboding incited by the terrorist attacks, King gathered supporters at a mass meeting at Bethel Baptist Church. While leading the large crowd in prayer, he got wrapped in emotion as never before. Speaking of the dangers that the protesters faced in the days and months ahead, he gripped the pulpit tightly and, his voice cracking, cried out, "If anyone should be killed, let it be me."[2]

He could not continue. Several ministers came to the pulpit and held him in their arms for several minutes.

Later, as King rushed around the city pleading for restraint, he was heartened by the reaction of the city's white leaders and press. The governor made an inspection of the damage and offered a reward for the capture of the bombers; the Montgomery *Advertiser* condemned the bombings in forceful terms; and white preachers rose in their pulpits to attack the bombings as un-Christian.

For Montgomery's black citizens, who had hung together through the long year of battle, this latest flourish of violence would also be overcome. One woman told a reporter, "Did you ever dream of getting a million dollars some day and buying all the things you've wanted? For us, now, it's like suddenly getting a million-dollar check ... we've waited a hundred years for it, only it's Friday afternoon and the bank won't open until Monday. It really doesn't matter if we don't get the cash until Monday. A weekend is not so long, now."[3]

Satisfied that the situation in Montgomery had stabilized, King and Abernathy returned to Atlanta to resume their meeting with 60 ministers from 10 southern states. Out of their deliberations came a ringing call for blacks to rise up in nonviolent protest to fight segregation and a call for President Eisenhower to visit the South and get behind these efforts. Eisenhower rejected that invitation.

At a subsequent meeting in New Orleans on February 14, the group formed the Southern Christian Leadership Conference (SCLC) and elected King as its first president.

Embodying the vision and philosophy of King, the SCLC would foster a mass movement based on the Christian tenets of love and understanding and become a major force in American politics. King and other SCLC leaders, mostly young Christian ministers, became indefatigable in rallying town after town and community after community to accept their strategy of confronting government and business power with nonviolent methods; to take on the always discouraging odds for the cause of racial justice and civil rights; to put behind them the taunts and threats of the mobs, the small defeats and large setbacks; and to keep on working, singing, and marching. From one town to another, from one set of circumstances to another, they would challenge the power with marches, boycotts, and sit-ins. They would take on southern segregation in an orderly, structured, and peaceful series of campaigns.

Working primarily in the South, as the name of the organization implied, the SCLC began to conduct leadership-training programs and citizen-education projects. Although King's personality dominated the organization, other activists were also prominent. They included Abernathy, King's closest associate; Andrew Young, of the National Council of Churches, who later became U.S. ambassador to the United Nations and mayor of Atlanta; Joseph Lowery, a Methodist minister from Montgomery who was named chairman of the board; and Ella Baker, a longtime promoter of community-based civil rights activism from Georgia.

In the weeks and months following the beginning of the Montgomery bus boycott, King had become an internationally recognized figure, not only for his stand on equal rights but for his insistence on nonviolent protest. In February, *Time* magazine, featuring a cover photo of King, ran a story called "Attack on the Conscience." It talked about this new black leader from Montgomery to whom other blacks across the South were beginning to look for the strategies and tactics to take on the evils of segregation: "The man whose word they seek is not a judge, or a lawyer, or a political strategist or a flaming orator. He is a scholarly, 28-year old Baptist minister ... who in little more than a year has risen from nowhere to become one of the nation's remarkable leaders of men."[4]

On May 17, 1957, three years to the day after the *Brown v. Board of Education* decision, King traveled to Washington, D.C., to participate with other civil rights leaders in a "Prayer Pilgrimage." Here, he delivered his first major national address, calling for black voting rights. On this day on the steps of the Lincoln Memorial, King's message clearly connected with the crowd, estimated by some at over 20,000. Six years later, King would return to the Lincoln Memorial in one of the most memorable moments in American history.

THE CRISIS AT LITTLE ROCK

In the fall of 1957, Little Rock, Arkansas, became the scene of the first major battle over the Supreme Court decision in *Brown v. Board of Education*. The Brown decision had struck down the doctrine of "separate but equal" (segregated schools could exist if both black and white schools were of equal quality) that had plagued reformers who wished for black children to be able to attend the same public schools as whites. The crisis that developed in Little Rock would test the limits of the Brown decision, set the stage for federal intervention in the civil rights movement, and pave the way for Martin Luther King and others to carry on a national movement, without fear of the abandonment of police protection for the rights of nonviolent protesters.

On the night of September 2, Governor Orville Faubus in a television address announced to the citizens of Arkansas that he was calling out the National Guard to keep peace and order. Nine black children who had wished to enter Little Rock's Central High School would be forced to leave, he declared. The school would remain segregated.

Faubus was in the first year of a second two-year term as governor of Arkansas. A relative political moderate, he was under attack by right-wing adversaries who were attempting to paint him as a liberal. The Little Rock school integration controversy seemed an ideal ticket out of political trouble. He began to give advice on tactics to anti-integration groups in the state. To his television listeners, Faubus said that information had reached his office that white supremacists were heading to Little Rock to disrupt integration attempts. If blacks attempted to enter Little Rock Central, he warned, the city's streets would run with blood.

As president of the Arkansas state conference for the NAACP, Daisy Bates had taken on the role of mentor, advisor, and strategist for the nine students. Her house became the gathering place and command post of the group, the pick-up and drop-off site for the students as they traveled to and from the school in the early days of the crisis. Members of the press knew they could follow events from the Bates house. It also became a frequent target of white protesters.

Although nearly 300 army and Air National Guard troops assembled at Central High, their presence held off the efforts of the black students for only a single day. Daisy Bates, other civil rights workers, and the students themselves would not be intimidated.

On September 4, ignoring Faubus's intimidation, she called to tell the students that they were to meet a few blocks away from the school and walk in together. The Arkansas National Guard, along with the police, successfully turned away the black students. As the *New York Times* reported, "Fully armed, the troops kept the Negroes from the school grounds while an angry crowd of 400 white men and women jeered, booed, and shouted, "Go home, niggers." Several hundred militiamen, with guns slung over their shoulders, carrying gas masks and Billy clubs, surrounded the school."[5]

The open defiance of school integration by the governor of Arkansas marked the beginning of a confrontation with federal and state authority and set the stage for a major test of the *Brown v. Board of Education* Supreme Court decision. Martin Luther King anxiously awaited the outcome. On September 9, King decided to use whatever strength his newly acquired position as a spokesman for civil rights could lend to the moment. He sent a wire to President Eisenhower warning that if the federal government did not take strong action to control the situation in Arkansas, that failure would set back the process of integration by 50 years.

Eisenhower's advisers and political reality echoed the sentiments King had sent. A few days later Eisenhower summoned Faubus to a meeting in Newport, Rhode Island where the president was visiting. On September 14, the two met and talked about the troubles in Little Rock. In the brief meeting, Eisenhower thought he had gained an agreement from Faubus that the black students would be enrolled. The president told Faubus that the National Guard troops could stay at Central High to protect the students.

By the time he returned to Arkansas, Faubus had decided on a new tactical maneuver. Contrary to what Eisenhower understood to be the agreement, Faubus ordered the troops to withdraw. The nine students would have only the Little Rock police for protection.

On September 23, the students again attempted to enter Central High. They faced a mob. Running a gauntlet of insults, taunts, and spit from the crowd, they managed to make it inside the building. On September 24, Little Rock Mayor Woodrow Mann, fearful that city police would be unable to maintain order, wired President Eisenhower. He asked for federal troops to protect the students.

Essentially pessimistic and passive about integration, Eisenhower agonized behind the scenes about an effective course of action. Extremely reluctant to use federal power against a state government, he nevertheless, realized that Faubus had forced his hand and that the situation in Little Rock was quickly spiraling out of control. Finally, he decided to take military action. First, he nationalized the Arkansas National Guard, removing it from Faubus's control. Then, he dispatched to Central High School 1,000 U.S. paratroopers from the 101st Airborne Division, a unit known as "The Screaming Eagles."

In sending troops to intervene, the president declared on national television, "The proper use of the powers of the Executive Branch to enforce the orders of a federal court is limited to extraordinary and compelling circumstances. Manifestly, such an extreme situation has been created in Little Rock. This challenge must be met and with such measures as will preserve to the people as a whole their lawfully protected rights in a climate permitting their free and fair exercise."

On September 25, accompanied by the crack paratroopers, the students arrived at the entrance of the school in an army station wagon. As an army helicopter circled overhead, the paratroopers stood at parade rest against an increasingly raging mob, many of them Central High students, many of them parents of Central High students, and others there merely to stoke the fires. As soldiers pushed back the mob and cleared the school halls, the nine students headed to their classes. During the first few days, each of the black students was assigned a personal guard from the 101st. Never before had federal troops been used to enforce integration in a public school.

Knowing that the actions of Eisenhower in Little Rock would set a critical precedent in the federal government's role in the civil rights movement, King again wrote to the president, "The pen of history will record that even the small and confused minority that oppose integration with violence will live to see that your action has been of great benefit to our nation and to the Christian traditions of fair play and brotherhood."[6]

As the great national showdown ended and the crowds dispersed and the cameramen and reporters gradually went on to other stories, the nine students were left to fend for themselves. Their own war went on. Their advisors, parents, and school officials told them not to physically or verbally retaliate against harassment or attacks. Instead, they were to report incidents to school authorities. They were, in other words, highly vulnerable.

A small but insistent group of whites took full advantage. They routinely beat up the black students, particularly the boys. They destroyed lockers and tried various avenues of intimidation, from rock throwing to ridicule. They sent notes to the black students threatening lynching. The black students and their families endured repeated angry and obscene phone calls at home. On several occasions, gunshots shattered windows of their houses. One student was even splashed in the face with acid.

Eight of the Little Rock Nine, one a senior, finished the school year. On May 27, 1958, students in the senior class of Central High joined in commencement ceremonies at Quigley Stadium. The event was protected by 125 federal troops and a contingent of city police. The days leading up to the graduation ceremonies sparked violence. Bates's house was firebombed, and Mayor Mann and his family received death threats and watched crosses burn on their lawn.

But on this graduation day, 601 students walked to the platform to receive their diplomas. Six hundred of the students were white. One was black. For Martin Luther King, Little Rock would be the prelude to other direct action protest confrontations.

BACK TO ATLANTA

For over two years King traveled back and forth from Montgomery to Atlanta, attempting to balance his responsibilities as pastor of Dexter Baptist Church, the increasing demands of the civil rights struggle, of which he was now such a major force, and his parental responsibilities. The King's second child and first son, Martin Luther III, was born in Montgomery on October 23, 1958. The couple's third child was due in January, 1961. They would name him Dexter.

Coretta told a reporter that the emotional and physical overload was taking a toll: "We like to read and listen to music, but we don't have time for it. We can't sit down to supper without somebody coming to the door … the pressure of this dulls you. Or perhaps you grow better prepared for anything."[7]

With the balancing act of responsibilities becoming increasingly intolerable, King and his wife realized that the time had come to accept his father's offer to return to Atlanta as a pastor at Ebenezer. Here he could rejoin his parents and close friends in his hometown; here he could carry on the work of the SCLC at its headquarters.

On November 29, 1959, in an emotional announcement to the congregation, King submitted his resignation as pastor of Dexter. "I want you to know," he said, "that after long and prayerful meditation, I have come to the conclusion that I cannot stop now. History has thrust upon me a responsibility from which I cannot turn away." As the congregation rose for the benediction and sang "Blest Be the Tie That Binds," King's eyes filled.[8]

THE SIT-IN MOVEMENT

In February, 1960, in Greensboro, North Carolina, four black students from North Carolina Agricultural and Technical College purchased items in the downtown Woolworth's store and sat down at the lunch counter. When told by a waitress to leave the whites-only counter, they explained that they had purchased items in the store and that they should be allowed to take a seat, rather than stand. When the manager of the store did not press the students to leave, they continued sitting for nearly an hour until the store closed.

The next morning the four students returned to the Woolworth's store, accompanied by more than 20 friends. When the national news learned of the protest, several stories appeared of well-dressed black college students attempting to assert basic human rights, and ending each day's protests with prayers. It took five months in Greensboro, months of bomb threats and clashes between protesters and white antagonists, as well as a boycott of stores with segregated lunch counters, but the protests produced results. Local officials agreed to negotiate store policies in return for an end of the demonstrations. The student sit-in movement was underway.

By year's end students would challenge segregation ordinances in over a hundred cities, not only in the South but in several northern cities as well. In Raleigh, North Carolina, police arrested over 40 students.

In Nashville, over 100 student protesters were herded from lunch counters to jail. Led by John Lewis and Vanderbilt Divinity School student James Lawson, the Nashville protests were especially well organized. It was Lawson, like King a student of Ghandian nonviolent resistance, who enlisted a number of the student leaders who would play larger roles in the civil rights movement in the coming years, including Marion Barry and Diane Nash. The Nashville movement was especially successful, as store after store desegregated their lunch counters.

At a mass meeting in Durham, North Carolina, attended by students from several states, King told them that they must be willing to "fill the jails." The sit-down movement, he told a reporter, "gives the people an opportunity to act, to express themselves, to become involved on the local level with the struggle."[9]

At Shaw University in Raleigh, North Carolina, several civil rights leaders, including Ella Baker, one of King's administrators for the SCLC, invited student sit-in leaders to a large meeting. Although the stated agenda was to discuss nonviolent resistance and ways to sustain their movement, Baker and others were convinced that the students should form their own organization. Over 200 students, mostly black, attended the meeting, representing several colleges and social reform organizations. Out of the meeting emerged the creation of the Student Nonviolent Coordinating Committee (SNCC).

Marion Barry became SNCC's first chairman, and other Nashville activists, including Lewis and Nash, would play important roles in the organization's early years. Baker soon left the SCLC for the new organization, although she remained an advisor to King and SCLC.

On October 20, 1960, King joined students at a sit-in at Rich's Department Store in Atlanta. Along with 13 others, he was arrested and jailed. In court he declared, "We did nothing wrong in going to Rich's today." The object of the demonstration, "he said, was to bring the whole issue of desegregation "into the conscience of Atlanta."[10]

FREEDOM RIDES

In 1960, the Supreme Court ruled in *Boynton v. Virginia* that segregation within interstate travel was illegal. This decision made segregation
in bus terminals, waiting rooms, restaurants, rest rooms, and other interstate travel facilities unconstitutional.

Shortly after the decision, two students from Nashville, John Lewis
and Bernard Lafayette, decided to test the ruling by sitting at the front
of a bus headed out of state. When the two encountered no serious
resistance, one national civil rights organization asked the two to lead
a more daring protest ride. The Congress of Racial Equality (CORE),
a civil rights organization founded following World War II and now
led by James Farmer, asked them to participate in a "Freedom Ride," a
longer bus trip through the South to continue testing the enforcement of
Boynton. Although Lafayette's parents would not allow their son to join
this potentially dangerous national confrontation, Lewis joined 12 other
young activists recruited by CORE. The group began extensive training
in nonviolent direct action of the kind exhibited so valiantly by blacks
during the Montgomery bus boycott.

On May 4, 1961, the first Freedom Riders left Washington, D.C.,
in two buses, one a Greyhound and the other a Trailways, and headed
south, scheduled to arrive in New Orleans, Louisiana on May 17, the
seventh anniversary of the *Brown v. Board of Education* Supreme Court
decision. The tactics were pointed and direct: the black students would
scatter throughout the buses. When the buses reached segregated rest
stops, some blacks would enter white facilities and some whites would
enter black ones.

The Freedom Riders not only expected to meet resistance; they were
courting it. The strategy was to incite incidents in which the federal
government would be compelled to enforce the law, as it had done in
the Little Rock integration struggle. CORE director James Farmer later
declared, "When we began the ride I think all of us were prepared for
as much violence as could be thrown at us. We were prepared for the
possibility of death."[11]

Although the riders met sporadic threats and incidents of violence in
the upper South, a special fury awaited in Alabama. The night before
they left Atlanta to head to Montgomery, King invited the riders to a
rally. He hailed their unbelievable courage and their attachment to a
cause greater than themselves. Privately, however, he harbored deep fears
that the following days might be the last for some of the young people.

On Mother's Day, May 14, 1961, the Freedom Riders split up into two groups to travel through Alabama. In Anniston, Alabama, one of the buses was greeted by a mob of about 200 yelling whites, armed with rocks, knives, iron pipes, and clubs. Surrounding the bus, the mob began hurling stones and slashing tires. Fearful of an imminent slaughter, the bus driver kept the vehicle moving, weaving around the mob, and continuing haltingly down U.S. highway 78. Lurching along with flat tires, the bus managed to get away temporarily but soon a few cars were on its tail.

When the driver finally stopped, several cars surrounded the bus and firebombed it. Some of the attackers tried to prevent the students inside from leaving the burning wreckage. As they forced their way out of the burning bus, the enraged whites pounded the students with various objects.

Finally, Alabama state troopers arrived, dispersed the melee, and took the injured students to a nearby hospital. A photograph of the burning bus, snapped at the scene, would later demonstrate to the world the kind of intense hatred that faced reformers who tried to break segregation in the American South.

The other group of bus riders met its own taste of retribution in Birmingham. After riders were beaten bloody at the Birmingham bus depot, Alabama's governor had only this to say, "When you go somewhere looking for trouble, you usually find it…. You just can't guarantee the safety of a fool and that's what these folks are, just fools." Strong evidence later surfaced that the police, the governor's office, and other local officials had purposely given free reign to members of the Ku Klux Klan to batter the demonstrators.[12]

The pure viciousness of the attacks stunned not only the riders themselves but also the bus companies. Neither Greyhound nor Trailways wanted anything more of the Freedom Rides; they feared for their drivers as well as for the buses themselves. Many of the injured riders left Montgomery by plane for New Orleans to recuperate and recover.

Into the breach stepped some familiar faces—the student protesters who had led the sit-down protests in Nashville, led by Diane Nash. The Nashville contingent agreed to continue the ride from Birmingham to Montgomery. She later explained: "If the Freedom Riders had been stopped as a result of violence, I strongly felt that the future of the movement was going to be cut short. The impression would have been that whenever a movement starts, all [you have to do] is attack it with massive violence and the blacks [will] stop."[13]

On May 17, the Birmingham police arrested the Nashville students and jailed them. It was, the police said, for their own protection. That pretense of protective custody was quickly shattered in the early morning hours. Waking the students in their cells, the police dragged them into vehicles, hauled them across the state line into Tennessee, and dumped them on the side of the road. Undaunted, the students did not head back to Nashville, as the Birmingham authorities assumed they would. The students walked railroad tracks, found the home of a black couple who gave them assistance, and located a driver who agreed to take them back to Birmingham. Squeezed into the car as close to the floor as they could manage, they were slowly driven by the back roads into Birmingham.

By now the cat-and-mouse game had turned even more deadly ominous. In Washington, a new Democratic administration under President John F. Kennedy had recently taken over the reigns of government. The Kennedy administration was understandably reluctant to charge into the civil rights fray. The Democratic Party still depended on the so-called Solid South for its power in Congress and the fragile majority it had mustered in the 1960 presidential election. Although personally sympathetic to the plight of black Southerners, Kennedy and his brother, Robert Kennedy, the Attorney General, were not about to plunge the Democratic party into fratricidal warfare over the race issue.

Nevertheless, Martin Luther King, a nearly peerless analyst of political behavior, believed that for blacks to exercise the power of nonviolent protest and to stamp the cause with overwhelming moral authority would make it increasingly difficult for the administration not to come down on the side of justice. He was right.

The racial battles over the Freedom Riders deeply worried Attorney General Kennedy. Fearful that scores of individuals would lose their lives if violence flared further in the Freedom Rides protest, Kennedy phoned a number of involved individuals and groups, including the Greyhound Bus Company.

The round of negotiations led to raucous meeting in the Birmingham office of Alabama Governor John Patterson, an avowed segregationist desperate to save his political career, and representatives sent by the Kennedy White House. During the negotiations, a cocky but fuming Patterson declared, "I've got more mail in the drawers of that desk over there congratulating me on the stand I've taken against what's going on in this country ... against Martin Luther King and these rabble-rousers. I'll tell you I believe that I'm more popular in this country today than John Kennedy is for the stand I've taken." Despite the governor's bluster, he did agree to protect the riders as they rode the highways of Alabama.[14]

On May 20, the ride from Birmingham to Montgomery, about 90 miles, was uneventful, except for the extraordinary sight of state patrol cars every 15 or 20 miles along the road, a police plane flying overhead, and scores of reporters, plainclothes state detectives, and FBI observers following behind in a bizarre convoy as the Greyhound bus barreled along at over 80 miles an hour.

When the bus reached Montgomery, however, the scene changed into an eerie silence. Suddenly there were no police. The terminal was empty. The riders soon realized they had been led into a trap, much like the one that the other riders had experienced back in Birmingham. "And then, all of a sudden, just like magic, white people everywhere," said Freedom Rider Frederick Leonard.[15]

As in Birmingham, many of the riders were beaten unconscious. Hundreds of whites chased the few riders down and inflicted damaging injuries. One of the most seriously injured was Jim Zwerg, a white rider. Also beaten severely was John Seigenthaler, an administrative assistant to Attorney General Kennedy and one of the representatives who had been sent to Birmingham by the administration to help keep the situation under control.

When news of the Montgomery attack reached Washington, Robert Kennedy was appalled. He sent federal marshals to the city.

On Sunday, May 21, King returned to Montgomery. About 50 federal agents met him at the airport and escorted him to the home of Ralph Abernathy. There, King and others made plans for a mass meeting that evening at Abernathy's church. In his speech, King thanked CORE for organizing the ride, praised the courage of the riders who faced ugly and threatening mobs, and compared the violence and barbarism of the white resisters to the reign of terror of Hitler's Germany. He placed the ultimate responsibility for the violence at the door of Governor Patterson and warned that if the federal government did not act to quell the violence the situation would degenerate into total chaos. He pledged that he and his organization would not sit idly by while black citizens of the South faced lawlessness and injustice.

"I strongly urge you to continue to follow the path of non-violence," he declared. "The freedom riders have given us a magnificent example of strong courageous action devoid of violence. This I am convinced is our most creative way to break loose from the paralyzing shackles of segregation. As we intensify our efforts in Alabama, Mississippi, and the deep South generally, we will face difficult days. Angry passions of the opposition will be aroused. Honesty impels me to admit that we are in for a season of suffering. I pray that recognizing the necessity of suffering we will make of it a virtue. To suffer in a righteous cause is to grow to our humanity's full stature. If only to save ourselves, we need the vision to see the ordeals of this generation as the opportunity to transform ourselves and American society. So in the days ahead let us not sink into the quicksands of violence; rather let us stand on the high ground of love and non-injury. Let us continue to be strong spiritual anvils that will wear out many a physical hammer."[16]

It took additional federal marshals to quell an ugly mob of hundreds outside the church where King gave his speech. The drifting stench of tear gas reached many blocks away.

On May 24, Kennedy ordered federal marshals to accompany the Freedom Riders to Mississippi. He negotiated an agreement with Mississippi Senator James Eastland that he would not use federal troops to oppose the segregation laws in this case if Eastland, through his influence with state officials, would make sure that the riders faced no violence.

There were no mobs this time at the bus station in Jackson, Mississippi. "As we walked through, the police just said, 'Keep moving' and let us go through the white side," recalled Frederick Leonard. "We never got stopped. They just said 'Keep moving,' and they passed us right on through the white terminal into the paddy wagon and into jail."[17]

More Freedom Riders arrived in Jackson to face arrest. By the end of the summer, hundreds had spent time in southern jails.

The Freedom Riders never made it to New Orleans. Some were physically scarred for life from the beatings they received. But their efforts had forced the Kennedy administration to take a stand on civil rights. The administration directed the Interstate Commerce Commission to ban segregation in any facilities under its jurisdiction, a much broader mandate than that covered by the recent Supreme Court decision regarding interstate transportation facilities.

For King, the rides were a testament of the will of young black Americans to break free of the shackles of segregation. It was this will, he knew, that would fuel the movement.

NOTES

1. Stephen B. Oates, *Let the Trumpet Sound: The Life of Martin Luther King, Jr.* (New York: Mentor, 1982), p. 106.

2. David Garrow, *Bearing the Cross: Martin Luther King, Jr. and the Southern Christian Leadership Conference* (New York: William Morrow, 1986), p. 87.

3. George Barrett, "Jim Crow, He's Real Tired," *New York Times Magazine*, March 2, 1957, p. 11.

4. "Attack on the Conscience," *Time*, February 18, 1957, p. 17.

5. Benjamin Fine, "Arkansas Troops Bar Negro Pupils; Governor Defiant," *New York Times*, September 5, 1957.

6. King to President Eisenhower, September 25, 1957, in Clayborne Carson, ed., *The Papers of Martin Luther King, Jr.*, vol. 4, http://www.stanford.edu/group/King/publications/papers/vol4/570925–002-To_Dwight_D._Eisenhower.htm.

7. Loudon Wainwright, "Martyr of the Sit-ins," *Life*, November 7, 1960, pp. 123–24.

8. Coretta Scott King, *My Life with Martin Luther King, Jr.* (New York: Holt, Rinehart and Winston, 1969), pp. 182–83.

9. "Integration: 'Full-Scale Assault,' " *Newsweek*, February 29, 1960, p. 25.

10. "14 Negroes Jailed in Atlanta Sit-Ins," *New York Times*, October 20, 1960, p. 39.

11. Juan Williams, *Eyes on the Prize: America's Civil Rights Years, 1954–1965* (New York: Viking Penguin, 1987, pp. 147–48.

12. "Freedom Rides," http://www.watson.org/~lisa/blackhistory/civilrights-55–65/freeride.html.

13. "Freedom Rides."

14. Taylor Branch, *Parting the Waters: America in the King Years 1954–163* (New York: Touchstone, 1988), pp. 441–42.

15. Williams, p. 153.

16. "*Speeches of Martin Luther King, Jr.*, Statement Delivered at a Rally to Support the Freedom Rides 21 May 1961, Montgomery, Alabama," http://www.stanford.edu/group/King/publications/speeches/unpub/610521–000_Statement_Delivered_at_a_Rally_to_Support_the_Freedom_Rides.html.

17. Williams, pp. 146–58.

Chapter 6

ALBANY, GEORGIA

Northern-bred merchant and entrepreneur Nelson Tift founded the town of Albany, Georgia in 1836, hoping it would become a major trade center, much like Albany, New York. Instead, over the years, cotton fields and pecan orchards surrounded the town. Indeed, Albany's pecans were the best in the country, at least in the view of Georgians. In 1961, Albany became the center of national attention—but not for its pecans.

Throughout the early 1960s, black students across the South, assisted by some whites, were making their protest voices heard in a number of ways—sits-ins, Freedom Rides, marches, and other nonviolent efforts to uproot segregation. In Albany three young civil rights workers, members of the Student Non-Violent Coordinating Committee (SNCC), arrived as part of an organizing effort to register black voters. As the three SNCC workers—Charles Sherrod, Cordell Reagon, and later in the year, Charles Jones—attempted to mobilize other students and local black leaders in the Albany area, they faced a particularly frustrating array of forces.

A city of about 50,000, Albany could boast, in addition to its agricultural products, a cherished isolation from other parts of the South that had already been swept up in this new drive against segregation. Although black individuals, most of them dirt-poor, represented about 40 percent of the town's population, and although it had within its city limits Albany State College, a state-run segregated institution for black students, Albany had yet to experience any of the turmoil intruding on its firmly established status quo. It had a strong-willed city government committed to resist any progressive challenges to its economic and social systems and its way of life. It also had a small, fairly well-to-do black professional class that enjoyed its privileged status. Nevertheless, with the arrival of SNCC, the tranquility of Albany was about to be tested.

The young SNCC organizers first concentrated their efforts on many of the 650 students at Albany State. They organized study groups and workshops, held meetings in black churches, and began to interest a sizable number of young people in joining the protest movement for civil rights.

Soon, Albany's black leadership sensed an opportunity for change. At first, a small committee of black representatives managed to set up a meeting with city leaders. Perhaps, they believed, some of the grievances could be negotiated. The meeting turned into a travesty when even some of their more moderate requests were defiantly rejected. The city was prepared even to ignore the Interstate Commerce Commission's order to ban segregated railway facilities. When the local newspaper, the Albany *Herald*, got wind of the attempted negotiations, it added its own condemnation of any proposed changes. Shortly thereafter, the home of one of the ministers involved with the black group was bombed. The fight was clearly on.

In mid-November, 1961, the major black organizations in the city founded a group called the Albany Movement and selected as their president William G. Anderson, a young black osteopath. The coalition, including the NAACP, community associations, and ministers, soon aimed their sights high. They would attempt to end all forms of racial segregation and discrimination in the city, from bus and train stations to libraries, food establishments, schools, parks, hospitals, jury representation, and public and private employment. And, in the course of the campaign, they would employ all of the direct action, nonviolent tactics they had seen or read about from other protests—sit-ins, boycotts, legal actions, marches, and mass demonstrations.

When several SNCC members were arrested attempting to use the whites-only waiting room facilities in the bus station, the response from the students, ministers, and others who had been part of the organizational efforts was overwhelming. Soon, student demonstrators were marching into whites-only facilities and joining the others behind bars. Within six weeks of the beginning of the demonstrations, approximately 2,000 students had filled Albany's jails.

Anderson, who had been a fellow student with Martin Luther King at Morehouse College, now decided to marshal all the national support he could to make Albany another successful stop on the road to civil rights. He asked King to join the Albany Movement.

On December 15, King, along with Ralph Abernathy, arrived in Albany. That evening, he spoke at the Shiloh Baptist Church. The next day he joined nearly 200 black citizens in a march and, along with them, was jailed on charges of parading without a permit, disturbing the peace, and obstructing the sidewalk. Abernathy and Anderson were also jailed.

Unlike the usual law enforcement authorities faced by King who inevitably played into his hands by overreacting, Albany Police Chief Laurie Pritchett was a special challenge. From the outset, it was clear that he was determined not to make the same public relations mistakes that had inflamed Montgomery and other towns and cities and given the black movement national attention.

Pritchett cautioned his police to treat demonstrators humanely, at least in public, and to avoid brutality and even name-calling. Conscious that King needed overreaction on the part of local authorities to fuel a successful outcome, Pritchett made every effort to counter King's nonviolence with nonviolence of his own. He would quietly enforce law and order without giving King and the ready cameras of the media the images of heartless, brutal racism. If King and his marchers wanted to become martyrs to police clubs, they would not do so in Albany, Pritchett was determined.

There would be no clubbing on the streets here, no crowds of threatening white mobs, no source of police outrage and misconduct from which the nonviolent protesters could get publicity and find common purpose. Instead, he simply directed the police department to round up demonstrators who violated local laws and herd them off to jail, not only in Albany itself but also in surrounding counties.

Not only students joined the movement. There were elderly men and women, individuals with medical and law degrees, laborers, and housekeepers, most of whom for the first time in their lives were now seeing the inside of a jail cell. But even though the jails were wretched and even though demonstrators suffered through the incarcerations, those scenes were not on public view, not as long as Pritchett could control the news.

Nevertheless, the appearance and jailing of King and other SCLC members in Albany lent immediate excitement and energy to the movement. Vernon Jordan, a young leader of the NAACP who was on the scene, later wrote: "King's arrest sparked the Albany movement. Everyone started marching and getting arrested—every day, it seemed that two hundred people would be arrested after breakfast, three hundred more after lunch, and two hundred more after dinner. Then every night there would be a mass meeting."[1]

King, Abernathy, and Anderson prepared to stay in jail until they had achieved some satisfactory agreement from city officials to overturn some of the city's segregation practices. Aware that King's presence in the city was turning the Albany Movement into a national story, city officials acted swiftly. They contacted some of the black officials and asked for a meeting.

On December 18, King was surprised by the news that some of the Albany Movement's leaders had reached a tentative agreement with city leaders. Without reading the details of the agreement carefully, King agreed to accept bail and leave jail. He soon realized he had been hoodwinked. The concessions by the city were neither broad nor secure. The so-called agreement was little more than a sham, a maneuver to persuade King to leave jail and to leave Albany.

After returning to Atlanta, King soon learned that the so-called agreement was largely ignored by city officials and he was embarrassed. Later, he wrote, "Looking back on it, I'm sorry I was bailed out. I didn't understand at the time what was happening. We thought that victory had been won. When we got out, we discovered it was all a hoax. We had lost a real opportunity to redo Albany, and we lost an initiative that we never regained."[2]

Nevertheless, King was determined to rejoin the protesters in Albany who carried on. They continued to hold sit-ins and marches and continued to court jail time. On July 10, King, Abernathy, and Anderson were again in court, this time drawing a sentence of 45 days.

A few days later, Coretta visited King. He wrote, "As usual Coretta was calm and sweet, encouraging me at every point. God blessed me with a great and wonderful wife. Without her love, understanding, and courage, 1 would have faltered long ago. I asked about the children. She told me that Yolanda cried when she discovered that her daddy was in jail. Somehow, I have never quite adjusted to bringing my children up under such inexplicable conditions. How do you explain to a little child why you have to go to jail? Coretta developed an answer. She told them that daddy has gone to jail to help the people."[3]

With King in jail, demonstrations and arrests increased. A few days later, Pritchett, realizing again that King's presence in jail was beginning already to mobilize the protesters, notified King and Abernathy that their bail had been paid and they were being released. King protested. He did not want another replay of the events the previous December when his exit from jail gave incorrect signals to the press that the problems in Albany had been settled. King argued that he could not be thrown out of jail against his will, regardless of whether the bail had been paid. He insisted on doing his time.

Pritchett ordered King to leave. Detectives drove King and Abernathy to Shiloh Church and dropped them off. King had essentially been kicked out of jail. He told reporters, "[T]his is one time that I'm out of jail and I'm not happy to be out.... I do not appreciate the subtle and conniving tactics used to get us out of jail."[4]

But this time, King vowed to stay in Albany until city officials backed away from their segregation policies. During the month following, the Albany Movement and city officials played something of a cat-and-mouse game. Protests and marches would be followed by jailings, several meetings, vague promises of reform, denials of promises—all leading to more protests. King and other leaders were themselves in and out of jail several times.

The Albany Movement suffered a brutal blow with a federal injunction banning King and his followers from protesting. This was not a local or state ordinance but an order from the federal government, and King was greatly distressed. Regularly in touch with Attorney General Kennedy about the succession of events in Albany, King had also wired the president on several occasions.

In late August two groups of white ministers arrived from Chicago and New York, hoping to meet with ministers and city officials to mediate the differences. After holding a prayer vigil, they were thrown in jail.

King sent a wire to Kennedy about the outrageous incident, saying that 15 Protestant and Jewish leaders were in jail and fasting "in hopes they will arouse the conscience of this nation to the gross violations of human dignity and civil rights, which are the rule in Albany and surrounding counties."[5]

King asked Kennedy to call representatives from the Albany City Commission and the Albany Movement together in Washington for a meeting to resolve the crisis. Even though seven U.S. Senators personally encouraged the White House to intervene in the situation, Kennedy did not arrange for such a meeting. The telegram was not acknowledged. Kennedy desperately wanted a cessation of the Albany protests. The awkward political situation into which the civil rights demonstrations had thrown the president seemed to be getting more devilish every day. He wanted it to end.

With the administration essentially backing out of the controversy, the Albany Movement suffered a grievous blow. Even though close to 95 percent of the black population boycotted buses and shops, even though more than 5 percent of the black population voluntarily went to jail, and even though the boycotts were economically damaging to the bus company and other merchants targeted by the protesters, the basic legal structure in Albany regarding segregation remained intact. King returned to Atlanta with national newspapers and magazines announcing that the racial barriers in Albany remained unbroken.

FBI SHADOWS

The days of the Albany protest had brought new elements to King and the movement. These were the days of the Cold War, of an escalating fear throughout the 1950s and into the 1960s of the domination of the Soviet Union and of communist infiltration not only in American society but also in the highest echelons of government. Government leaders and the media talked of the threat of nuclear weapons and the uncharted horrors that could lie ahead. Americans engaged in civil defense drills and built homemade bomb shelters. They watched the U.S. Congress interrogate Americans about their possible links to communist groups. They watched as writers and Hollywood personalities were paraded before inquisitors. They read in magazines and newspapers about the progress being made to devise new chemical and biological weapons. They read of the dire prospects of the world's population doubling before the end of the century bringing with it poverty, disease, and new recruits for the communist regimes. They wanted protection and intelligence, and they trusted the Federal Bureau of Investigation (FBI) and its power-wielding leader, J. Edgar Hoover.

If traitors were infiltrating the nation's highest offices, if communist leaders around the globe were arming against and aiming at the United States, where was the real protection for the average citizen? Hoover and his force were there. And now, the FBI had Martin Luther King, Jr. in its sights.

Over the years, the file on King at the FBI headquarters in Washington would grow larger and larger, filling up with information about his movements, friends, correspondence, plans, speeches, philosophy, and family.

The FBI began shadowing King's activities and those of the SCLC in 1961. It learned that one of King's most trusted advisors was Stanley Levison, a man with close ties to the Communist Party. In October 1962 the FBI opened a formal investigation of King and the SCLC under an FBI program captioned "COMINFIL"—meaning communist infiltration. Investigations under this program involved legitimate noncommunist organizations that the FBI believed were being influenced by Communist Party members. The bureau sought to find out the degree of infiltration of communists associating with King and whether King himself harbored communist sympathies or connections.

Soon, the bureau placed wiretaps in Levison's and King's homes and on their office phones, and they bugged King's rooms in hotels as he traveled across the country. The FBI also informed Attorney General Kennedy and President Kennedy, both of whom unsuccessfully tried to persuade King to dissociate himself from Levison. King adamantly denied having any connections to communism, stating at one point that "there are as many Communists in this freedom movement as there are Eskimos in Florida"—to which Hoover responded by calling King "the most notorious liar in the country."[6]

King's cavalier dismissal of Hoover and the FBI investigation further spiked the director's ire at the civil rights leader. King complained that the FBI notoriously worked alongside the city police and local officials against black protesters in a number of civil rights protests. Hoover was convinced that King was an immoral instigator of lawless actions, a communist sympathizer, if not an actual worker for the party. Hoover took great pains to keep his agents on the prowl, to notify the attorney general and the president of any suspicious behavior, and even sent tape recordings to government leaders purportedly showing King as a womanizer who partied often and hard. For the rest of King's life, Hoover crusaded to bring King down in the public's eye and to wreck his civil rights activities.

The extent to which the open hostility between the FBI and King had flared is reflected in one of the bureau's efforts to contact King. When Cartha D. DeLoach, head of the FBI's Crime Records Division, made a telephone call to the SCLC office in Atlanta, secretaries promised to ask King to return the calls. When King did not respond, DeLoach wrote in an FBI memo, "It would appear obvious that Rev. King does not desire to be told the true facts. He obviously used deceit, lies, and treachery as propaganda to further his own causes…. I see no further need to contact Rev. King as he obviously does not desire to be given the truth. The fact that he is a vicious liar is amply demonstrated in the fact he constantly associates with and takes instructions from [a] … member of the Communist Party." The war between King and the FBI would grow more vicious and demeaning.[7]

AN A CAPPELLA MOVEMENT

King and the movement had also found something else in Albany. It found its singing voice. Andrew Young, a new leader of the SCLC fresh from the National Council of Churches, began to organize citizenship workshops for the students and other protesters. Young set up nightly meetings and rallies at Shiloh Baptist Church. It was during these sessions, Young later remembered, that they found "an uncut diamond among the Albany students in sixteen-year-old Bernice Johnson." At one of the first meetings, she and other teenagers began to sing. Bernice's voice, Young wrote later, "was as rich as the soil around Albany, with the texture of all the suffering of black folk that made the crops grow."[8]

At Mt. Zion Baptist Church, Bernice Johnson, Ruth Harris, and Cordell Reagon formed the "Freedom Singers." Their a cappella singing led the way in giving a new dimension to the civil rights movement.

Ain't gonna let nobody, Lordy, turn me 'round,

turn me round, turn me 'round.

Ain't gonna let nobody, Lordy, turn me 'round.

I'm gonna keep on a-walkin', Lord,

marching up to freedom land.[9]

After Albany, Young remembered, the civil rights movement was more of a singing movement. There were such freedom songs as "We'll Never Turn Back," written by Bertha Gober in honor of Rev. George Lee, an NAACP leader who had been murdered in Mississippi because he refused to take his name off a voter registration list.

The music was an extension of the spirituals sung by slaves in the fields a century earlier. Now, young civil rights workers adapted the music for the times. Bernice Johnson later recalled the way in which singing evolved as an important tool during the struggle: "activist song leaders made a new music for a changed time. Lyrics were transformed, traditional melodies were adapted and procedures associated with old forms were blended with new forms to create freedom songs capable of expressing the force and intent of the movement."[10]

From those spirituals, hymns, and labor songs, such favorites as "Woke Up This Morning With My Mind on Freedom," "We Shall Not Be Moved," and "We Shall Overcome" now rang out along the lines of marchers and demonstrators from one end of the country to the other, refrains from people determined not to be denied.

LESSONS

When King looked backed on the events in Albany, he was both frustrated and a little wiser regarding the civil rights struggle. On reflection, he saw that his efforts in Albany had been too diffuse, that the attempt virtually to desegregate the city in all respects was far too vague and encompassing. It would have been a much more strategically sound campaign, he thought later, to attack a single aspect of the entrenched policies in the city, rather than attempt, as they did, a scattergun effort to strike all of the segregation edifice down in a single blow. "We attacked the political power structure instead of the economic power structure. You don't win against a political power structure where you don't have the votes. But you can win against an economic power structure when you have the economic power to make the difference between a merchant's profit and loss."[11]

He was also beginning to realize that his own celebrity was becoming an increasing factor that he must carefully consider as he selected his targets and planned for later campaigns. The press had now anointed King as the major figure in the civil rights movement. For thousands of workers who had walked the lines, gone to jail, and, especially for those leaders of other civil rights organizations, King's ascension to this lofty position was tenuous, and, for some, annoying. Many of the students, for example, thought he was too conservative in his tactics.

After King returned to Atlanta, many of the students carried on. But even though the Albany Movement had not reached the expectations of its leaders, even though lunch counters remained segregated, thousands of Negroes had been added to the voting registration rolls. Later, the library was opened on a 30-day trial basis to all citizens, black and white, and the City Commission repealed the entire section of the city code that carried segregation ordinances.

Charles Sherrod, one of the men who began the protests in Albany, later remarked, "Now I can't help how Dr. King might have felt, or ... any of the rest of them in SCLC, NAACP, CORE, any of the groups, but as far as we were concerned, things moved on. We didn't skip one beat."[12]

Peter de Lissovoy, one of the SNCC campaign workers in Albany, later remembered what his friends called "The Great Tift Park Pool Jump." With the change in segregation policies on the way and public facilities to be opened to blacks, the city sold its municipal swimming pool, named after the city's founder, to a private individual. The pool, therefore, would not be subject to the new integration ordinances.

"Everybody said we ought to just go on down and jump in and have a swim," said de Lissovoy. "This would first require scaling a steel fence. It was a hot summer. One morning about 75 kids took off from all directions bent on thus slipping through the alleys and byways and converging on Tift Park Pool. When we got there, though, only three had the nerve to hit that steel fence and go over—Randy Battle, Jake Wallace, and James Daniel. It truly appeared that when they hit the water, all the whites in the pool were sprung straight into the air onto the deck. They were so astounded and beside themselves with the impropriety that Randy, Jake, and James just walked out of the park and never got arrested."

There was an obvious mischievous nature of the event Peter de Lissovoy described. But when he talked about the pool jump years later, he also remembered the serious nature of the protests of the Albany Movement and the dangers involved. "People got killed for doing things like the Great Pool Jump in those days," he said.[13]

When King himself later assessed the events of Albany, he wrote, "To the Negro in the South, staggering under a burden of centuries of inferiority, to have faced his oppressor squarely, absorbed his violence, filled the jails, driven his segregated buses off the streets, worshiped in a few white churches, rendered inoperative parks, libraries, and pools, shrunken his trade, revealed his inhumanity to the nation and the world, and sung, lectured, and prayed publicly for freedom and equality—these were the deeds of a giant. No one would silence him up again. That was the victory which could not be undone. Albany would never be the same again."[14]

Reverend Prathia Hall agreed. After participating in a number of mass meetings in Albany churches, Hall said, "I was profoundly impacted by the Albany movement and the southwest Georgia project conducted by SNCC. It was my first experience of the deep South ... the very first night, there was a mass meeting. The mass meeting itself was just pure power ... you could hear the rhythm of the feet, and the clapping of the hands from the old prayer meeting tradition ... people singing the old prayer songs ... there was something about hearing those songs, and hearing that singing in Albany in the midst of a struggle for life against death, that was just the most powerful thing I'd ever experienced."[15]

NOTES

1. Vernon E. Jordan, *Vernon Can Read: A Memoir* (New York: Basic Books, 2001), p. 161.

2. "Man of the Year: Never Again Where He Was," *Time*, January 3, 1964, p. 15.

3. Clayborne Carson, ed., *Autobiography of Martin Luther King, Jr.*, (New York: Warner Books, 1998), p. 158.

4. David Garrow, *Bearing the Cross: Martin Luther King, Jr. and the Southern Christian Leadership Conference* (New York: William Morrow, 1986), p. 203.

5. Martin Luther King, Jr. to President John F. Kennedy, August 31, 1962, John F. Kennedy Library, Boston, Massachusetts.

6. "Supplementary Detailed Staff Reports on Intelligence Activities and the Rights of Americans. Book III, Final Report of the Select Committee to Study Governmental Operations with Respect to Intelligence Activities.

Dr. Martin Luther King, Jr. Case Study," http://www.icdc.com/~paulwolf/cointelpro/churchfinalreportIIIb.htm.

7. "Supplementary Detailed Staff Reports."

8. Andrew Young, *An Easy Burden: The Civil Rights Movement and the Transformation of America* (New York: HarperCollins, 1996), p. 171.

9. "Mt. Zion Baptist Church," http://www.cr.ps.gov/nr/travel/civilrights/g3.htm.

10. "Sweet Chariot: The Story of the Spirituals—Freedom Songs of the Civil Rights Movement: Slave Spirituals Revived," http://cctl.du.edu/spirituals/freedom/civil.cfm.

11. "Man of the Year," p. 15.

12. Lee W. Formwalt, "Moving forward by recalling the past …," http://members.surfsouth.com/~mtzion/movementhistory.htm.

13. Peter de Lissovoy, "Returning to Georgia," http://www.reportingcivlrightgs.org/perspectives/delissovoy.jsp.

14. Carson, p. 169.

15. "A Faith Forged in Albany," http://www.pbs.org/thisfarbyfaith/journey_4/p_4.html.

A young boy stands next to a segregated drinking fountain on the county court-house lawn in Halifax, North Carolina. April 1938. Courtesy of the Library of Congress.

Martin Luther King Jr. and wife, Coretta stand outside the Montgomery, Alabama courthouse. March 1956. Courtesy of the Library of Congress.

King—pictured here with his son, Marty—removes a burned KKK cross from his front lawn. April 1960. Courtesy of the Library of Congress.

Alabama Governor, George Wallace—defying a court order to admit black students to the University of Alabama—confronts Assistant U.S. Attorney General, Nicholas Katzanbach. June 1963. Courtesy of the Library of Congress.

King delivers the "I Have a Dream" speech on the steps of the Lincoln Memorial, Washington, D.C. August 28, 1963. Courtesy of the National Archives.

Civil Rights leaders gather at the "March on Washington" rally. August 28, 1963. Courtesy of the National Archives.

While attempting to march to Montgomery, Civil Rights leader, John Lewis is assaulted by Alabama state troopers. 1965. Courtesy of the Library of Congress.

King (left) and Ralph Abernethy (directly behind King) kneel before they are arrested during a demonstration in Selma, Alabama. 1965. Courtesy of the National Archives.

*Martin Luther King Jr.
at podium. Courtesy of
the Library of Congress.*

*King gives a fiery speech
at Girard College,
Philadelphia. 1965.
Courtesy of the Library
of Congress.*

Chapter 7

BLOODY BIRMINGHAM

The history of the civil rights movement can be traced by the names of southern cities that were the sites of major confrontations—Montgomery, Alabama; Little Rock, Arkansas; Albany, Georgia. And now, for King and his SCLC lieutenants, it was Birmingham, Alabama.

The largest iron and steel center of the South, Birmingham had attracted many black workers who had previously labored in the fields. Although they were not paid as much as white workers, they made far greater wages in the steel mills than on the farms. The great influx of black workers prompted white leaders, determined not to lose power and control, to enforce a rigid, strict segregation system. All public facilities were segregated, from restrooms and parks to taxicabs and department store fitting rooms.

Here, King said, was the most segregated city in the nation. In 1962, Birmingham's city parks and public golf courses had been closed to prevent desegregation. When black activists protested the city's racial policies by boycotting selected Birmingham merchants, city officials cut food supplies appropriated for needy families.

The city was one of the last remaining strongholds of the KKK. City businessmen, although embarrassed by the notoriety of Klan activities and the city's national infamy for racial segregation, remained intimidated and did nothing. Birmingham's police force, led by Police Commissioner Eugene "Bull" Connor, was fiercely anti-black and not about to give ground against protesters. When the Freedom Riders were attacked in Birmingham, the police were absent from the scene. The KKK had even pressured the city to ban a book containing pictures of black and white rabbits from bookstores. It was pushing the city government to ban black music on radio stations.

More seriously, bombings by the Klan and other white vigilante hate groups became so common in one middle-class black neighborhood of Birmingham that it became known as "Dynamite Hill." In eight years, the city had witnessed over 20 bombing incidents at homes, businesses, and churches. Civil rights activists estimated that at least a third of Birmingham's police officers were members or open sympathizers of the KKK.

King knew that any civil rights campaign in Birmingham would almost certainly provoke intense trouble. In other words, Birmingham was the ideal city for King to gain national attention. As Wyatt Tee Walker, one of King's lieutenants, explained: "We've got to have a crisis to bargain with. To take a moderate approach, hoping to get white help, doesn't work. They nail you to the cross, and it saps the enthusiasm of the followers. You've got to have a crisis."[1]

King and his leadership called the Birmingham plan "Project C." The "C" stood for confrontation. It was a strategy of nonviolent direct action designed to confront segregation through peaceful demonstrations, economic boycotts, and national appeals to human justice. It all hinged upon the reaction of Bull Connor. From all that King knew about his history and the reputation of the Birmingham police force, Connor would almost certainly play into his hands.

Unlike the events in Montgomery and Albany, King and his SCLC aides set out a carefully laid-out plan to turn Birmingham into a turning point in the civil rights movement. In early 1963, he met with local leaders, recruited over 200 individuals willing to go to jail for the cause, conducted workshops in nonviolent protest techniques, and announced publicly that he would lead demonstrations until "Pharaoh lets God's people go."[2]

At the same time, in January 1963, George Corley Wallace was inaugurated Alabama's governor in the Capitol of Montgomery. Short, with jet-black hair, Wallace threw his shoulders back during his inaugural speech and reminded his cheering admirers that he was standing on the same spot that Jefferson Davis had taken his oath of office as president of the Confederacy a hundred years earlier. Reaching the end of his oration, the new governor declared, "From the cradle of the Confederacy, this very heart of the great Anglo-Saxon Southland, I draw the line in the dust and toss the gauntlet before the feet of tyranny. And I say, Segregation now! Segregation tomorrow! Segregation forever."[3]

King would now answer Wallace's challenge. From January through March 1963, he traveled across the country, delivering speeches in 16 cities about the injustices of segregation and the need to take direct action against them. Although he did not reveal his plans for Birmingham, he was laying the groundwork, alerting the nation, the press, and government leaders that a major confrontation lay ahead. This would be a drama, King knew, that would be played out on a national stage.

In late March he hurried home to Atlanta where Coretta gave birth to their fourth child, a daughter they named Bernice. For much of their lives since the Montgomery bus boycott, the growing family had lived without King at home. With the upcoming struggle looming in Birmingham, Coretta realized that in the coming months and years the dilemma would undoubtedly be ongoing.

At SCLC headquarters, King and his staff readied for battle. At one of the planning meetings for Birmingham, King warned his colleagues about the extreme danger that he saw ahead. "I have to tell you in my judgment," he said, "some of the people sitting here today will not come back alive from this campaign. And I want you to think about it." It was something that King himself would think about constantly as the movement grew. There were groups and individuals that would go to any lengths to stop the protesters, especially in Birmingham, Alabama.[4]

THE CITY OF BULL CONNOR AND FRED SHUTTLESWORTH

Born into a working class family in Selma, Alabama in 1897, Eugene "Bull" Connor had worked as a telegrapher and radio sports announcer before entering state politics. In 1957, when he won the post of commissioner of public safety in Birmingham, Connor made it clear that he was segregation's firm defender. "These laws," he declared, "are still constitutional and I promise you that until they are removed from the ordinance books of Birmingham and the statute books of Alabama, they will be enforced in Birmingham to the utmost of my ability and by all lawful means."[5]

He meant what he said. The unsolved bombings, the coziness of the police force with the KKK, and his hair-trigger temper and bluster, bordering on buffoonery, all testified to that.

On the other side of Bull Connor was Reverend Fred Shuttlesworth, equally uncompromising in his commitment to civil rights as the police commissioner was to his commitment to power and the status quo. The two seemed made for conflict.

Raised in a rural, black community, educated at Selma University and Alabama State Teachers College, Shuttlesworth became a Baptist minister, first serving a church in Selma and later in Birmingham at the Bethel Baptist Church. In 1956, he founded the Alabama Christian Movement for Human Rights (ACMHR), an organization focused on direct action and committed to ending segregation in Birmingham. He helped King found the SCLC and was also deeply involved in organizing the Freedom Rides. Feisty, defiant, Shuttlesworth had nearly become a legend in Birmingham, taking on the city leadership as well as the KKK on civil rights issues.

In December 1956, when he brashly announced that Birmingham's buses would be henceforth desegregated and that black citizens would begin sitting in the front of buses, a bomb destroyed his home on Christmas Eve. Shuttlesworth was sitting in the edge of his upstairs bedroom when the bomb exploded, collapsing the home into a heap of rubble. Incredibly, Shuttlesworth emerged only slightly injured.

James Roberson, a young member of the church, said later, "Think about it. The police said eight to eighteen sticks of dynamite went off within three feet of this man's head. He's not deaf, he's not blind, he's not crippled, he's not bleeding. That really made me think he had to be God-sent." Much of Birmingham's African American community would, like James Roberson, thereafter see Shuttlesworth as a God-ordained leader. As Shuttlesworth put it, "That's what gave people the feeling that I wouldn't run ... and that God had to be there.[6]

Over the years, he was assaulted by police dog's, knocked unconscious by high-pressure fire hoses, and jailed. But he talked of the coming triumph of the black community: "Countless Negroes went to jail and lost their jobs. Some even lost their homes, and many left for other cities. The thousands of crank and very real telephone threats, the mobs at Terminal Station, and at Phillips Hight School, before which I was dragged and beaten in the streets and my wife stabbed in the hip; the two dynamite explosions, through which we lived by the grace of God ... the brutal tactics unleashed upon us by the city—all of these things did not move us, nor deter us from our goal."[7]

In May 1962, King and other SCLC leaders joined Shuttlesworth and the ACMHR in a massive direct action campaign to attack segregation in Birmingham. They believed that while a campaign in Birmingham would surely be the toughest fight yet of the civil rights movement, it would, if successful, have profound implications. The larger goal in Birmingham was to nationalize the movement, to force action from the Kennedy administration to push through Congress a comprehensive Civil Rights

Act that would outlaw segregation in public accommodations, employment, and education. The specific demands of the protest would be to
desegregate stores, to force fair hiring practices by the stores, to open up
fair employment for blacks in the city government, and to open municipal
recreational facilities on an integrated basis.

In early April 1963, King and the SCLC, in league with Suttlesworth's
local organization and other black leaders, began lunch counter sit-ins,
marches on City Hall, and a boycott of downtown merchants. With the
onset of the protests, black volunteers increased and so did the protest
sites. There were sit-ins at the main library, a march on the county building to open a voter registration drive, and demonstrations at churches.
"We did not hesitate to call our movement an army," King said.[8]

On April 7, Bull Connor and the Birmingham police responded in the
way King and his lieutenants had assumed that he would. He brought
out the dogs. As King's brother, A. D., led a band of protesters, news
photographers snapped pictures of the snarling canine corps rushing on
long leashes toward the protesters. One dog reached a man and pinned
him to the ground, as other protesters rushed in to help. The photograph
appeared the next day in a number of newspapers around the country.
The fight was on.

On April 10, the city government obtained a court injunction demanding an end to the protests, a move anticipated by King. As he and the
SCLC had planned, they would defy the court order and begin their
inevitable arrests and jail time.

LETTER FROM BIRMINGHAM'S JAIL

On Good Friday, April 12, 1963, hundreds of people waited in and
around Sixteenth Street Baptist Church for King to lead 50 volunteers
on a march that was certain to culminate in their arrest. To rhyth-
mic clapping of supporters lining both sides of the march, with police
barricades waiting, they headed toward Bull Connor. As the police
commissioner shouted orders for their arrest, King, along with Ralph
Abernathy, knelt in prayer. Both were seized and thrown in paddy wag-
ons, along with the other marchers.

Andrew Young, one of King's closest allies, later wrote: "Connor ordered
his police to go after the bystanders, and attempt to clear the park. Using
nightsticks to jab people in the ribs, and with snarling and snapping dogs
straining on their leashes, the police line advanced relentlessly on the
demonstrators.... Amid the confusion and terror, SCLC staff members
tried to guide people into the Sixteenth Street Baptist Church." Inside,

Young pleaded with King's supporters to avoid retaliation. They listened, accepted his entreaties, and left the church singing "Ain't gonna let nobody turn me 'round, keep on a-walkin, walking up to freedom's land."[9]

King was kept in solitary confinement and allowed little direct contact with anyone. His request to call Coretta was denied. After two days, King's jailors became suddenly more accommodating. He was permitted to see his attorneys and to call Coretta. Fearing for his safety, she had spoken with both President Kennedy and Attorney General Robert Kennedy. The White House asked city authorities to ensure King's safety.

C. Virginia Fields, a young high school student in Birmingham at the time of King's arrest, later remembered: "When you saw the kind of things that were carried out against people based purely on the color of their skin, yeah, it made you angry. And it made you resentful and at some point you felt like it was all white people. That there was no difference. Everybody is not like Bull Connor, but at some point all white people become Bull Connor. It is that simple." Nevertheless, when word reached Birmingham that King was coming to join the marchers, she said, there was euphoria in the air that swept through the black community. When King was in the city jail, Fields was in there also.[10]

While King remained in jail, singer Harry Belafonte helped raise the necessary funds to provide bail for those arrested. During the first days after King's arrest, several prominent white clergymen took out a full-page newspaper ad criticizing King's protest movement in Birmingham and charging him with inciting unnecessary and ill-timed troublemaking.

The ad struck a nerve deep in King. These were religious men standing four-square against what King sincerely believed was a moral and religious stand of the first order, a fight for justice and equality that stood at the core of Christian commitment.

On April 16, 1963, King began a response on the margins of a newspaper that he had in his cell and continued to write on scraps of paper given to him by a fellow inmate who had become a trusty. Eventually, he concluded the letter on a pad that his attorneys were finally allowed to give to him. Addressed to "My Dear Fellow Clergymen," the letter traced the road that drove him and others to Birmingham to join with black citizens in attacking the life-sapping segregation engrained in the city's laws and customs.

He was in Birmingham, he said, not as an outside agitator but as an American citizen, concerned, as any citizen should be, about injustice in any part of the country. He went on to attack the idea that change would come within the natural order of progress. Change, he argued, must be earned by those willing to sacrifice for the common good.

He defended the tactic of direct action and the right of the civil rights movement to defy the law. He talked about the long suffering and humiliation that an entire people had endured, of the codified hatred embedded in the segregation laws, and of the immediacy of the cause. When you see policemen attack your black brothers, when you see 20 million blacks smothering in poverty, King said, when you "seek to explain to your six-year-old daughter why she can't go to the public amusement park that has just been advertised on television, and see tears welling up in her eyes when she is told that Funtown is closed to colored children, and see ominous clouds of inferiority beginning to form in her little mental sky, and see her beginning to distort her personality by developing an unconscious bitterness toward white people; when you have to concoct an answer for a five-year-old son who is asking: 'Daddy, why do white people treat colored people so mean?'; when you take a cross-county drive and find it necessary to sleep night after night in the uncomfortable corners of your automobile because no motel will accept you; when you are humiliated day in and day out by nagging signs reading 'white' and 'colored'; when your first name becomes 'nigger,' your middle name becomes 'boy' (however old you are) and your last name becomes 'John,' and your wife and mother are never given the respected title 'Mrs.'; when you are harried by day and haunted by night by the fact that you are a Negro, living constantly at tiptoe stance, never quite knowing what to expect next, and are plagued with inner fears and outer resentments; when you are forever fighting a degenerating sense of 'nobodiness,' then you will understand why we find it difficult to wait."[11]

Pieced together and published in its entirety in newspapers around the country, King's letter gave confidence to millions of blacks who were frustrated and ready for change; its eloquence and careful argument gave voice and understanding to his cause.

King was released from Birmingham's jail on April 20.

THE CHILDREN'S MAY CRUSADE

Despite the national impact that the Birmingham demonstrations had commanded, the SCLC found it difficult by late April to sustain the protest. The Birmingham battle became one of numbers; could King and his allies continue to overwhelm Birmingham law enforcement agencies with streams of protesters willing to go to jail? In fact, the movement was in jeopardy of running out of such volunteers.

In order to maintain pressure, King and his SCLC organizers made an agonizing decision. Several of King's workers had commented on the enthusiasm and dedication shown by local college and even some high school students in the events transpiring in the city. In an unprecedented and high-stakes strategy decision, the leaders decided to encourage students to become a force for change. The word spread quickly. Hundreds of high school students streamed into workshops on nonviolence held by King's aides. In many cases, they brought their younger brothers and sisters. King saw them as freedom fighters in a cause for their own future. They felt the same way.

On May 2 over 1,000 children and teenagers gathered at the Sixteenth Street Baptist Church for what protest leaders called "D-Day." By nightfall, Bull Connor had arrested 959 of them. A thousand children missed school the next day.

That night, another thousand young people packed the church and listened to King exhort the youngsters to remain calm and courageous. The following morning, as the young protesters gathered at the Sixteenth Street Church, Connor ordered the church sealed. Half of the children were trapped inside; others made it out and gathered across the street in Kelly Ingram Park. Police charged into the park, beating numerous youngsters and some bystanders. Connor turned dogs on them. Many adult onlookers, who previously had felt afraid to protest, now began throwing bottles and bricks.

Connor then ordered up the fire hoses and city firemen obliged. With television cameras rolling, the hoses pelted hundreds of pounds of water pressure into the crowd, knocking bricks off walls, ripping the bark off trees, and sending people sliding and falling.

Americans across the country watched the spectacle on television. This was not some foreign land; this was not a motion picture; this was a major American city. In only two days, some 1,300 black children were thrown in jail. The police beatings, water hosing, and dog attacks, rising to national headlines, increased with tremendous power the pressure on the Kennedy administration and Birmingham's civic leaders to act.

Clearly angered at his administration's political dilemma over civil rights, Kennedy was, nevertheless, repulsed by a photograph on the front page of the *New York Times* showing a 15-year-old black child being attacked by one of Connor's police dogs. Speaking to a friend on the phone, Kennedy said, "There is no federal law that we could pass to do anything about that picture in today's *Times*. Well there isn't. I mean what law can you pass to do anything about police power in the community of Birmingham? There's nothing we can do. There's no federal law to support us. No federal statute. There's no federal law we can pass. Now the fact of the matter is Birmingham is in the worst shape than any city in the United States and it's been that way...."[12]

Kennedy sent Burke Marshall, his chief civil rights assistant, to facilitate negotiations between the SCLC and representatives of Birmingham's business and political community. A Yale Law School graduate and committed civil rights advocate, Marshall proved to be a valuable negotiator between the protesters and city officials. King associate John Lewis said, "He, perhaps more than any other person during the Kennedy and Johnson years, was one person you could call on. He was the one person you could rely on."[13]

On May 4, round-the-clock negotiations began between activists and city officials, but neither side gave ground. The demonstrations escalated as did the police brutality. Robert Holmes remembers how as a teenager he and his brother once had to physically restrain their father from rushing downtown to shoot the dogs. Robert Holmes, Sr., who dug ditches for the Alabama Gas Company, saw on the news the demonstrators fleeing German shepherds and bolted for the door. "We held him because we didn't want him to be killed," said his son.[14]

On May 6, attendance dropped 90 percent in some schools and another 1,000 people were arrested. "The jails could not hold us," Fred Shuttlesworth said later. "Over 3,000 Blacks, mostly high school kids ... filled the jails; and the world was watching."[15]

On May 7, even more people took to the streets, sitting in at lunch counters, marching, singing, and chanting. At lunchtime in downtown Birmingham, students tied up traffic for several square blocks. Connor's police trapped 4,000 people in Ingram Park and again turned the hoses on them. Very few individuals were hustled off to jail because there was no place to put them.

Shuttlesworth was among the many protesters who were swept off their feet by blasts from fire hoses. Suffering from chest injuries, Shuttlesworth was carried off by ambulance to the hospital. When told that his arch-rival had been taken away in an ambulance, Bull Connor said, "I wish they had taken him away in a hearse."[16]

With Burke Marshall continuing to lead marathon discussions between the protesters and white business, professional, and civic leaders, the two sides reached a breakthrough on May 10. White businesses made some concessions to black demands, although not nearly as comprehensive as King had wished. Nevertheless, since King found it increasingly difficult to restrain his followers from violence, he accepted the deal and declared victory, announcing at a press conference that all public facilities would be desegregated and that city officials would reverse discriminatory hiring practices. He also announced the formation of a committee to ensure nondiscriminatory hiring practices in Birmingham, and continuing negotiations between black and white leaders to maintain public peace and calm.

Clearly upbeat about the national exposure and the success at Birmingham, King said, "Activities which have taken place in Birmingham over the last few days to my mind mark the nonviolent movement coming of age." This was the first time in years of the civil rights movement, he said, when "we have been able literally to fill the jails. In a very real sense, this is the fulfillment of a dream."[17]

When the agreement was made public, white extremists acted quickly, making clear their determination never to negotiate away the social system in place. They set off a bomb at the home of King's brother, the Reverend A. D. King. They planted a bomb near the Gaston Hotel where King and other leaders of the SCLC were lodged. Birmingham was again living up to the name given to it by a number of civil rights leaders—Bombingham.

At the White House in Washington, President Kennedy, in order to ward off the escalating violence, ordered 3,000 federal troops into position near Birmingham and made preparations to federalize the Alabama National Guard. An uneasy calm set in.

For seven days in May, the vivid contrast had been there for the world to see—helmeted policemen wielding sticks and leading attack dogs against black children. The incidents in Birmingham moved Kennedy to remark, "[T]he civil rights movement should thank God for Bull Connor. He's helped it as much as Abraham Lincoln."[18]

In the three months that followed the momentous days in Birmingham, there were nearly 1,000 individual boycotts, marches, and sit-ins in about 200 cities across the South. They became known as "Little Birminghams."

The dogs and the streams of water that knocked over scores of men, women, and children on the streets of Birmingham proved the efficacy of King's strategy of nonviolent confrontation. Despite the pain and injuries and overwhelming indignities suffered, the protesters prevailed. Responding to the White House's experience in dealing with the Birmingham protests, President Kennedy began to work on broad civil rights legislation to Congress, which would eventually lead to the passage of the Civil Rights Act of 1964.

King and his allies had fought in the belly of the segregation beast. They had demonstrated that urgent change was necessary, just, and possible.

NOTES

1. "Man of the Year: Never Again Where He Was," *Time*, January 3, 1964, p. 16.

2. "Man of the Year," p. 16.

3. Stephen B. Oates, *Let the Trumpet Sound: The Life of Martin Luther King, Jr.* (New York: New American Library, 1982), p. 206.

4. David Garrow, *Bearing the Cross* (New York: Vintage Books, 1988), p. 229.

5. William A. Nunnelly, *Bull Connor* (Tuscaloosa: University of Alabama Press, 1991), p. 61.

6. Tim Stafford, "A Fire You Can't Put Out: Remembering Martin Luther King, Jr.," http://www.christianitytoday.com/books/web/2001/jan17a.html.

7. Peter B. Levy, ed., *Documentary History of the Modern Civil Rights Movement*, (Westport, Conn.: Greenwood Press, 1992), p. 116.

8. Oates, p. 210.

9. Andrew Young, *An Easy Burden* (New York: HarperCollins, 1996), pp. 216–20.

10. Randal C. Archibold, "Fields Carries Faith, Consensus and Civil Rights Roots to a Mayoral Bid," *New York Times*, August 23, 2005.

11. "Martin Luther King's Letter from Birmingham Jail," http://www.citadel-information.com/mlk-letter-from-birmingham-jail.pdf.

12. James Warren, "Thoughts from the Past; Newly Released JFK Oval Office Tapes Reveal His Frustration over Civil Rights Movement," *Chicago Tribune*, January 17, 2005, p. 19.

13. Marlon Manuel, "Civil Rights 'Racial Peacemaker' Dies, Marshall, 80, was JFK's Top Law Strategist," *The Atlanta Journal-Constitution*, June 4, 2003, p. A11.

14. "Up from Jim Crow," *Newsweek*, September 18, 2000, p. 42.

15. Ronald Carson, "An Interview with the Rev. Fred Shuttlesworth," *Call and Post*, August 12, 2004, p. 1.

16. "Rioting Negroes Routed by Police at Birmingham," *New York Times*, May 8, 1963, p. 28.

17. "Rioting Negroes Routed."

18. Nunnelly, p. 164.

Chapter 8

TUMULT AND TRAGEDY—1963

As King returned to Atlanta in mid-May 1963, he was determined that the success in Birmingham must be followed by additional pressure, that he must continue to persuade the Kennedy administration to take an active role in the civil rights struggle and to submit to Congress federal civil rights legislation. He began publicly to admonish the administration for its failure to speak to the country about an enormous issue that needed to be addressed. In one interview, King said that President Kennedy "has not furnished the expected leadership."[1]

As King contacted civil rights leaders around the country to plan for the next steps of the civil rights campaign, racial storms continued to rage in Alabama.

MOVING WALLACE AWAY FROM THE SCHOOLHOUSE DOOR

While campaigning for the governorship of Alabama in 1962, George Wallace told campaign rallies that if the Kennedy administration attempted to integrate his state's schools, "I shall refuse to abide by any such illegal federal court order even to the point of standing in the schoolhouse door." Wallace's rhetoric stirred the voters, and he easily prevailed in the election.[2]

On June 11, 1963, at the University of Alabama in Tuscaloosa, on the steps of Foster Auditorium, Wallace kept his campaign promise. As Vivian Malone and James Hood attempted to register as the first two black students, Wallace, his head thrown back, stood at the door defying a federal court order.

But Wallace would not stop integration that day in Alabama. The Kennedy administration, realizing that a governor could not be allowed to defy the federal courts, was also there on the steps, in the person of Deputy Attorney General Nicholas Katzenbach, who was flanked by federal marshals.

When Wallace affirmed the constitutional right of the states to operate public schools, colleges, and universities, Katzenbach asserted the necessity of the state to adhere to federal court orders. Katzenbach told Wallace that the students would be registered that day.

Katzenbach, the students, and the marshals walked down the steps to ease the situation for the moment. When Katzenbach called President Kennedy to discuss the impasse, Kennedy federalized the Alabama National Guard and insisted that Wallace step aside.

Although both President Kennedy and Attorney General Robert Kennedy had engaged in private conversations with Wallace and his associates about the confrontation, and even though Kennedy felt certain that Wallace would back down, Kennedy had prepared for the physical removal of the governor. Kennedy had ordered the guard to practice how physically to lift Wallace by the armpits out of the doorway with as little force as possible. If all this was theatrics, it was theatrics on a grand scale, on national television. It was imperative that the administration be seen as upholding the law with resolve and dignity.

Having made his political statement and not wanting to be whisked bodily away from the scene, the governor finally stepped aside and left Tuscaloosa for his office in Montgomery. The two students entered the building to register for classes. Vivian Malone later said her goal was simply to sign up for accounting classes. "I didn't feel I should sneak in, I didn't feel I should go around the back door. If [Wallace] were standing at the door, I had every right in the world to face him and to go to school." Two years later, she became the first black student to graduate from the University of Alabama.[3]

On that evening at 8:00 P.M. in Washington, President Kennedy faced the television cameras for a national address. Much like President Eisenhower had done six years earlier after he sent troops to Little Rock, Kennedy explained why Alabama's National Guard had to carry out the admission of the two students. "We are confronted primarily with a moral issue," he said. "It is as old as the scriptures and is as clear as the American Constitution. The heart of the question is whether all Americans are to be afforded equal rights and equal opportunities, whether we are going to treat our fellow Americans as we want to be treated. If an American, because his skin is dark, cannot eat lunch in a restaurant open to the public, if he cannot send his children to the best public school available, if he cannot vote for the public officials who will represent him, if, in short, he cannot enjoy the full and free life which all of us want, then who among us would be content to have the color of his skin changed and stand in his place? Who among us would then be content with the counsels of patience and delay?"[4]

Kennedy announced that he would ask the Congress to make a commitment in law that race has no legal place in American life. He would ask Congress to authorize the federal government to participate more fully in lawsuits designed to end segregation in public education.

Kennedy's moral appeal to conscience, his declaration of rights, King believed, was a great step forward for the civil rights movement. He called it "the most earnest, human and profound appeal for understanding and justice that any President has uttered since the first days of the Republic."[5]

This was the development for which King and his supporters had worked—a presidential bill to provide national civil rights protections. The confrontation with Wallace, closely following the events in Birmingham, had forced the administration to take action. King knew that the critical moment in the civil rights struggle had arrived. He prepared for the biggest demonstration of all—a march to Washington.

MARCHING ON WASHINGTON

For A. Philip Randolph it was a long time coming. In 1941, Randolph, the president of the Brotherhood of Sleeping Car Porters, had planned a march on Washington, designed to pressure the Roosevelt administration to guarantee jobs for blacks in armament industries crucial to the war effort. Randolph canceled the march when President Roosevelt issued an executive order barring discrimination in defense industries and federal bureaus. It was the first executive order protecting black rights since the Emancipation Proclamation. After the war Randolph was also a central figure in persuading President Harry S Truman to ban racial discrimination in the military.

At the end of 1962 Randolph, now one of the leaders of the AFL-CIO, began to discuss with civil rights organizer Bayard Rustin of the SCLC the possibility of staging a big Washington demonstration. Rustin had been involved two decades earlier in the original plan for the march. The two talked now about forming a coalition of organizations and unions that would gather in the nation's capitol to rally and lobby the White House and Congress for social and economic civil rights goals.

On July 2, at New York's Roosevelt Hotel, King met with Randolph and Rustin, along with Roy Wilkins of the NAACP, James Farmer of CORE, John Lewis of SNCC, and Whitney Young, Jr. of the Urban League to establish a march organization.

Dubbed the "March on Washington for Jobs and Freedom," the event would stress economic inequities and press for a new federal jobs program and a higher minimum wage. But now, with President Kennedy pressing for a civil rights bill, the march would take on a new dimension. The gathering would represent the largest lobbying group ever to mass in the nation's capitol.

Working feverishly out of a makeshift office in Harlem, Rustin handled the complicated logistics of a gathering that would involve hundreds of organizations and thousands of people. As civil rights leaders fanned out across the country they carried with them an organizing manual prepared by Rustin, and they began to hold meetings in numerous cities and towns preparing for the trek to the nation's capitol.

By August 17, march organizers had sold nearly 200,000 official buttons for the occasion as well as photograph portfolios with such images as protesters being hosed by Bull Connor's men in Birmingham. At Harlem's Apollo Theatre such jazz luminaries as Quincy Jones, Herbie Mann, and Thelonious Monk hosted a celebrity fundraiser. Writer James Baldwin and movie actor Burt Lancaster led a march in Paris in support of the Washington event.

Uneasy about the possibility of violence breaking out in the heart of Washington, D.C., President Kennedy was less than keen on the planned march and tried to persuade the leadership to cancel it. He argued that such a demonstration might alienate the very members of Congress whose votes he needed to pass his civil rights legislative agenda. When it became clear that his argument was failing to persuade any of the organizers, Kennedy decided to publicly laud the goals of the march.

Washington authorities and march organizers were determined to ensure a peaceful day. The District of Columbia police units had all their leaves canceled; neighboring suburban forces in Maryland and Virginia practiced riot-control. The Justice Department worked with army coordinators on possible emergency troop deployments; Fifteen thousand paratroopers were put on alert. Liquor sales were banned for a day, the first time since Prohibition. Two Washington Senators' baseball games were postponed. All the anxiety about violence would soon evaporate. The thousands who came that day were not interested in trouble; they were there peaceably to assemble. A *New York Times* writer called it "A Gentle Army."[6]

Most marchers came in buses chartered by local branches of the movement; another 30,000 or so arrived in 21 chartered trains. Members of CORE's Brooklyn chapter walked the 230 miles to the march in 13 days. On August 28, the day of the march, New York's Penn Station officials said the crowd was the largest seen there since the end of World War II. About 15 percent of the participants were students and about 25 percent were white. Estimates of the crowd ranged from 200,000 to 500,000. One young man completed a weeklong journey from Chicago on skates. He wore a sash that read "Freedom." Another young black teenager bicycled to Washington all the way from South Dakota. It was unquestionably the largest political demonstration in the history of the United States.

The United Auto Workers union, one of the march's biggest sponsors, printed hundreds of signs with slogans such as "UAW Says Jobs and Freedom for Every American." A young man from the South, undoubtedly a veteran of the many protests that had followed Birmingham, carried a handwritten sign that said. "There Would Be More of Us Here but So Many of Us Are in Jail. Freedom Now."

While march leaders were meeting with congressional representatives on Capitol Hill, at the Washington Monument marchers gathered in front of a stage set up for morning entertainment. Joan Baez opened with "Oh Freedom" and also led a rendition of "We Shall Overcome." Other performers included Odetta, Josh White, and Bob Dylan.

Press representatives from around the world gathered on the mall. At a large tent near the Lincoln Memorial, the march committee issued over 1,500 press passes. Large crews of reporters and photographers and television cameramen fanned out from the Capitol, where demonstrators met with their elected representatives; to nearby Union Station where trains carrying groups from across the country bounded into the station waving placards, and singing the old spiritual "We Shall Not be Moved"; to the Washington Monument, where celebrities such as Marlon Brando, Paul Newman, Ossie Davis, Harry Belafonte, Peter, Paul, and Mary, and Odetta gathered; to the White House to get reaction from administration spokesmen to the event; and to the Lincoln Memorial, where the central gathering would take place under the majestic statue of the president who had become an icon for blacks in the United States.

Charles Dolby, age 4, from Detroit, perhaps best expressed the feelings of the thousands who made their way to the mall. Fresh off the train, Charles was asked by one of the reporters where he was going and what was he going to do there. He said simply, "Get some more freedoms."[7]

The march was one of the first events to be broadcast live around the world via the communications satellite Telstar. CBS covered the rally throughout, preempting such daytime favorites as "Art Linkletter's House Party," "To Tell the Truth," and "As the World Turns."

As the ceremony began at the Lincoln Memorial, Bayard Rustin introduced to the roaring crowd Rosa Parks, Daisy Bates, Diane Nash, and other women who had been so instrumental in the movement. Marian Anderson, who had years earlier been prohibited by the Daughters of the American Revolution from singing at Constitution Hall because of her race and who, through the work of Eleanor Roosevelt, had performed instead at the Lincoln Memorial, was back to sing "He's Got the Whole World in His Hands."

As the major speakers began their appearances, Roy Wilkins warned President Kennedy to withstand attempts to water down the civil rights bill. Whitney Young's speech, which focused on urban inequities, was addressed to future black marchers. John Lewis's rousing speech was interrupted loudly and often with applause and shouts. Mahalia Jackson sang the gospel classic, "I've Been 'Buked and I've Been Scorned." And now it was time for King. By the time he mounted the platform, both ABC and NBC had cut away from their programming to join CBS in covering the event. King would be speaking to nearly the entire national television audience.

Most of those watching on television had never listened to King's oratory. They had seen news clips of the protest marches, heard his remarks about civil rights developments, and perhaps heard short snippets of speeches. Now, for the first time, Americans across the country could witness what his early teachers had seen in this remarkable speaker, could feel the passion and depth of his message, could roll with the rhythms and intensity of his words. As he reached his speech's final crescendo, it was clear why this young minister had already made such a national impact. "When we allow freedom to ring," he declared, "when it rings from every village and every hamlet, from every state and every city, we will be able to speed up that day when all God's children, black men and white men, Jews and Gentiles, Protestants and Catholics, will be able to join hands and sing in the words of the old Negro spiritual: Free at last! Free at last! Thank God Almighty, we are free at last."[8]

Sitting behind King, Coretta marveled at the reaction. "As Martin ended," she wrote, "there was the awed silence that is the greatest tribute an orator can be paid. And then a tremendous crash of sound as two hundred and fifty thousand people shouted in ecstatic accord with his words."[9]

As the marchers left the Washington Mall, King and the other leaders gathered at the White House to discuss with President Kennedy strategy on the pending civil rights bill. Following the meeting, Kennedy issued a statement on the march that began: "We have witnessed today in Washington tens of thousands of Americans—both Negro and white—exercising their right to assemble peaceably and direct the widest possible attention to a great national issue.... What is different today is the intensified and widespread public awareness of the need to move forward in achieving these objectives—objectives which are older than this nation."[10]

As the crowd withdrew, Bayard Rustin noticed his long-time friend A. Philip Randolph standing alone at the dais. He walked over and put his arm around the old man's shoulder and said, "Mr. Randolph, it looks like your dream has come true." Randolph replied that it was "the most beautiful and glorious day of his life." Rustin saw tears streaming down his friend's face.[11]

While sitting by a government building waiting for her bus to take her back home, Mrs. Hazel Mangle Rivers said, "If I ever had any doubts before, they're gone now. When I get back home I'm going to follow this on out. I've followed it this far. When I get back there tomorrow, I'm going to do whatever needs to be done—I don't care if its picketing or marching or sitting-in or what. I'm ready to do it." Mrs. Rivers was headed back to Alabama with great purpose.[12]

BOMBING THE INNOCENT

Looking back on the summer and fall of 1963, King wrote later, "It would have been pleasant to relate that Birmingham settled down after the storm, and moved constructively to justify the hopes of the many who wished it well. It would have been pleasant, but it would not be true. After partial and grudging compliance with some of the settlement terms, the twentieth-century night riders had yet another bloodthirsty turn on the stage."[13]

Two weeks after the August 28, 1963, March on Washington for Jobs and Freedom, the Sixteenth Street Baptist Church in Birmingham, the largest black church in the city, prepared for Youth Sunday. On September 15, the children's choir would perform for the congregation, children would serve as ushers, and the preacher would deliver a sermon especially geared for young persons. For many of the youngsters, the summer had been one of excitement, fear, and, most of all, participation. Many of them had marched with King for civil rights, had been splattered and flattened by streams from the fire hoses, had faced the teeth of police dogs, and had been jeered and cursed by mobs of whites. Their courage and suffering had jolted the nation, from the president of the United States to the average American watching the news on television.

For members of the KKK and other whites resistant to social change in Birmingham, Sixteenth Street Baptist represented a house of the devil. It was in the church that Martin Luther King, Fred Shuttlesworth, and other civil rights leaders had planned their next moves; it was from the church that they would march across the street to Kelly Ingram Park to hold demonstrations against segregation and racism. To the KKK Sixteenth Street Baptist was a target.

As the parishioners prepared for the church service on that Sunday morning, a bomb made of at least 15 sticks of dynamite sat beneath a stone staircase along the outside wall of the church and in close proximity to the basement of the Byzantine-style structure, with its two domed towers. It had been placed there several hours earlier and timed to explode when the church was full of worshippers.

When the bomb exploded, walls buckled and blew out, stone and debris flew like shrapnel through the basement, and stained glass windows shattered, their colored glass whistling throughout the church like missiles. The only stained glass window in the church that remained in its frame showed Jesus leading a group of little children. The face of Jesus was blown out. Songbooks lay shredded and scattered through the church. The blast crushed two nearby cars and blew out house windows blocks away.

Mamie Grier, superintendent of the Sunday School, said when the bomb went off "people began screaming, almost stampeding" to get outside. The wounded walked around in a daze, she said. Dozens of parishioners dripping blood staggered through the rubble and the white, stifling dust.[14]

But the most grievous sight was in the basement. After the police dispersed the hysterical crowds and workmen with pickaxes grimly dug through the chunks of concrete and other wreckage, they found, amidst pieces of brightly painted children's furniture and books, the bodies of four young girls. The blast had killed Denise McNair, 11 years old, and Cynthia Wesley, Carole Rosamond Robertson, and Addie Mae Collins, all 14 years of age. The four children were in the dressing room in the church basement when the bomb, apparently hidden beneath the church steps the night before, detonated at 10:19 A.M., as the children were assembling for closing prayers following Sunday school classes. Some 400 people were in the church at the time. Mamie Grier was the last adult to see the girls alive, as they excitedly talked about the beginning of the new school year.

Carolyn McKinstry, who was 14 years old at the time, was secretary of her Sunday school class. She was taking attendance records into the sanctuary when the bomb went off. "I heard something that sounded, at first, a little like thunder and then just this terrific noise and the windows came crashing in," McKinstry told National Public Radio in 2001. "And then a lot of screaming, just a lot of screaming and I heard someone say, 'Hit the floor.' And I remember being on the floor…and it was real quiet."[15]

Reverend John Cross, his church emitting a white fog of ash and steeped in rubble of brick and concrete, made his way to the steps of the church to plead with a gathering crowd for calm. When a Civil Defense worker handed him a megaphone, Cross shouted, "We should be forgiving as Christ was forgiving as He hung from the cross.…"[16]

But as word of the bombing swiftly reverberated around the black communities of Birmingham, thousands began to make their way toward the church. Police units, fearing a full-scale riot, patrolled the area, as National Guardsmen stood ready at an armory. Some blacks began to stone cars and gunshots rang both from police and blacks. Soon, the death toll rose, as police shot to death a 16-year-old boy when he refused to stop throwing stones at cars and a 13-year-old boy on a bicycle was shot and killed when he ignored police orders.

King quickly wired George Wallace that "the blood of four little children … is on your hands. Your irresponsible and misguided actions have created in Birmingham and Alabama the atmosphere that has induced continued violence and now murder." Only a week before the bombing, the governor had said that to stop integration Alabama needed a "few first-class funerals."[17]

King also wired President Kennedy: "I shudder to think what our nation has become when Sunday school children … are killed in church by racist groups. The savage bombing of the 16th Street Baptist Church this morning is another clear indication of the moral degeneration of the State of Alabama and Governor George Wallace. Mr. President, you must call for legislation."[18]

For the Klan, the bombing was a victory. White supremacist leader Connie Lynch, speaking to a meeting of Klansmen, said those responsible deserved medals. Lynch said that the four young girls who were killed "weren't children. Children are little people, little human beings, and that means white people."[19]

The towering irony in the Birmingham protest was that a church bombing, meant to intimidate demonstrators, instead galvanized the civil rights workers, the press, the public, and a new, if still reluctant, civil rights booster in the White House. Yachting off Newport, Rhode Island, when the bombings occurred, President Kennedy, when notified of the tragedy, realized more clearly that the White House would find it increasingly difficult to play the middle ground and attempt to placate both sides. The four dead girls in a church basement had turned Birmingham into a cause that could not be finessed.

On September 18, King had the painful responsibility of eulogizing the slain children, "These beautiful children of God." Innocent, unoffending, they died, he said, as martyrs for a cause of justice. As incomprehensible and tragic as their deaths, perhaps they served as redemptive forces from which justice and freedom could rise. He said: "They have something to say to every minister of the gospel who has remained silent behind the safe security of stained-glass windows. They have something to say to every politician [Audience:] (Yeah) who has fed his constituents with the stale bread of hatred and the spoiled meat of racism. They have something to say to a federal government that has compromised with the undemocratic practices of southern Dixiecrats (Yeah) and the blatant hypocrisy of right-wing northern Republicans. (Speak) They have something to say to every Negro (Yeah) who has passively accepted the evil system of segregation and who has stood on the sidelines in a mighty struggle for justice. They say to each of us, black and white alike, that we must substitute courage for caution. They say to us that we must be concerned not merely about who murdered them, but about the system, the way of life, the philosophy which produced the murderers. Their death says to us that we must work passionately and unrelentingly for the realization of the American dream."[20]

Justice would come slowly—agonizingly slowly—for the perpetrators of the bombing. The FBI had early information that the bombing had been carried out by a splinter group of the KKK known as the Cahaba Boys. Four men, evidence suggested, were responsible for the atrocity—Robert Chambliss, known as "Dynamite Bob," Herman Cash, Thomas Blanton, and Bobby Cherry.

After a witness identified Chambliss as the man who placed the bomb at the Sixteenth Street Baptist Church, he was arrested and charged with murder and possessing a box of 122 sticks of dynamite without a permit. On October 8, 1963, he was found not guilty of murder by a jury of his peers and received a hundred-dollar fine and a six-month jail sentence for possession of dynamite.

According to a 1980 Justice Department report, J. Edgar Hoover, a fervent opponent of the civil rights movement, had blocked prosecution of the Klansmen even though his agents had obtained evidence. In 1968 Hoover shut down the investigation without filing charges. Gary T. Rowe, an FBI informant active in the Birmingham KKK, told the Senate Select Committee on Intelligence that the FBI had known of and condoned his participation in violent attacks against blacks.

Nevertheless, 14 years after the bombing, in November 1977, Alabama authorities, led by a vigorous attorney general named Bill Baxley, once again opened the case against Dynamite Bob Chambliss. This time, now aged 73, he was found guilty on state murder charges and sentenced to life imprisonment. He died in an Alabama prison eight years later.

It was not until May 2000 that the bombing case would again be reopened, this time to charge Chambliss's accomplices. Cash was already dead but both Blanton and Cherry were arrested.

Thirty-eight years after the bombing, Thomas Blanton, Jr. was finally convicted of murder and sentenced to life in prison. A year later, in May 2002, Bobby Cherry was also found guilty for the deaths of the four girls, and given a sentence of life in prison. In the courtroom that day, when the last of the verdicts was finally handed down, was a man who had seen and felt all of it Birmingham—Fred Shuttlesworth.

In looking back over the rocky cliffs of highs and lows that had marked 1963, Reverend C. T. Vivian of Atlanta, one of Dr. King's closest comrades-in-arms and a top leader of the SCLC, who was with King in Birmingham, said later. "No one who is involved in a struggle for freedom and justice dies in vain. We are all part of the whole. We all gain our sense of freedom based on how we respond to the death and suffering of anyone who stands for those freedoms."[21]

King himself said later that the summer of 1963 "was historic partly because it witnessed the first offensive in history launched by the Negroes along a broad front. The heroic but spasmodic slave revolts of the ante-bellum South had fused, more than a century later, into a simultaneous, massive assault against segregation."[22]

As the mountaintop of the Lincoln Memorial merged into history with the ashes of the Sixteenth Street Baptist Church, King struggled against heavy forces on all sides to keep the movement on track, to reject calls for violent reaction, and to convince officials in the Washington power structure finally to come to grips with the nation's most pressing issue.

NOTES

1. David Garrow, *Bearing the Cross* (New York: Vintage Books, 1988),p. 267.

2. "George Wallace," http://www.spartacus.schoolnet.co.uk/USAwallaceG. htm.

3. Debbie Elliot, "Wallace in the Schoolhouse Door," http://www.npr.org/templates/story/story.php?storyId=1294680.

4. "Radio and Television Report to the American People on Civil Rights, President John F. Kennedy, June 11, 1963," http://www.jfklibrary.org/j061163.htm.

5. Stephen Oates, *Let the Trumpet Sound* (New York: Mentor, 1982), p. 238.

6. "200,000 March for Civil Rights in Orderly Washington Rally; President Sees Gain for Negroes," *New York Times*, August 29, 1963.

7. "Rallies at Way Stop Cheer Thousands on March Trains," *Washington Post*, August 29, 1963.

8. *New York Times*, August 29, 1963.

9. Coretta Scott King, *My Life with Martin Luther King, Jr.* (New York: Holt, Rinehart and Winston, 1969), p. 240.

10. "Texts of the President's Statements on Rights...." *New York Times*, August 29, 1963.

11. Thomas Gentile, *March on Washington: August 28, 1963* (Washington, D.C.: New Day Publications, 1983), p. 250.

12. "Marcher from Alabama," *New York Times*, August 29, 1963.

13. Clayborne Carson, ed., *Autobiography of Martin Luther King, Jr.* (New York: Warner Books, 1998), p. 229.

14. "Six Dead After Church Bombing," *Washington Post*, September 16, 1963.

15. "16th Street Baptist Church Bombing: Forty Years Later, Birmingham Still Struggles with Violent Past," National Public Radio, All Things Considered, http://www.npr.org/templates/story/story.php?storyId=1431932.

16. Diane McWhorter, *Carry Me Home* (New York: Simon & Schuster, 2001), p. 525.

17. "Six Dead After Church Bombing."

18. Martin Luther King, Jr. to President John F. Kennedy, September 15, 1963, John F. Kennedy Library

19. *Free at Last: A History of the Civil Rights Movement and Those Who Died in the Struggle* (Southern Poverty Law Center, 2004), pp. 56–57.

20. "Eulogy for the Young Victims of the Sixteenth Street Baptist Church Bombing, delivered at Sixth Avenue Baptist Church," http://www.stanford.edu/group/King/speeches/pub/Eulogy_for_the_martyred_children.html.

21. Tim Wheeler, "Four Little Girls: Promises Still Unmet," *People Weekly World Newspaper*, June 1, 2002, http://www.pww.org/article/view/1295/1/88/.

22. Oates, p. 247.

Chapter 9

JOHNSON, KING, AND THE CIVIL RIGHTS ACT OF 1964

On November 22, 1963, King was home in Atlanta. Upstairs, with the television in the background, King heard the news. President Kennedy had been shot in Dallas, Texas, perhaps fatally. He called to Coretta, who was downstairs on the phone, and she rushed up to watch the unfolding news. When it was announced that the president had died, King, who had been very quiet, said to Coretta, "This is what is going to happen to me also. I keep telling you, this is a sick society." She had no words of comfort. As she wrote later, "I felt he was right. It was a painfully agonizing silence. I moved closer to him and gripped his hand in mine."[1]

Outside Washington, D.C., on the tarmac at Andrews Air Force Base, President Lyndon Johnson, who had been sworn into office while on Air Force One, faced the nation for the first time since the tragedy. "This is a sad time for all people," he said. "We have suffered a loss that cannot be weighed. For me it is a deep personal tragedy. I know the world shares the sorrow that Mrs. Kennedy and her family bear. I will do my best. That is all I can do. I asks for your help and God's."[2]

Terrible circumstances had changed America's course and also that of the civil rights movement. King, whose insistent pressure and confrontational tactics had forced a national spotlight on the issues surrounding race relations in the United States and had helped persuade an anxious and reluctant Kennedy to take positive action on civil rights legislation, now faced the prospect of dealing with a southerner in the White House. What was King to make of this new challenge; what was he to make of the rangy, craggy Texan under whose stewardship presidential action on civil rights would be directed?

Six feet, four inches tall, with a prominent nose, large ears, and squint-eyes, the new President, a former Senator with a long, distinguished career, was oversized in many important respects—ego, appetite, legislative instincts, and a mastery of persuasion. His ability to convince a senator or member of the House to swing to his side of an issue was legendary. Cagey, insistent, tireless, he invaded space, bending over and down on those his wished to persuade, getting close to their face, while reeling off homilies and humor, facts and supposition. On the phone, he was just as formidable, calling at all hours, arguing and cajoling at a breathless pace.

Although the Kennedys had held Johnson at length, repulsed by his brusque and common manner, the new president was basically comfortable with many of the leftward-leaning policies espoused by the Kennedy administration. With a philosophy rooted in Franklin Roosevelt's New Deal, Johnson saw government as a positive vehicle for reform, an answer to many of the problems facing average Americans. Although Johnson had not emphasized civil rights legislation in his career, King was hopeful that his political background and instincts would lead toward reform. The civil rights leader was determined to enlist Johnson's support for the movement.

Little did King know that just hours after he had become president, Johnson talked in the early-morning hours with his close friend Jack Valenti. When he began thinking of the direction he wished to take, Johnson told an astonished Valenti, "I'm going to pass the civil rights bill and not change one word of it. I'm not going to cavil, and I'm not going to compromise. I'm going to fix it so everyone can vote, so everyone can get all the education they can get." Johnson himself, King would soon learn, saw the civil rights cause not only as just but as one that could be won.[3]

Bottled up by powerful southern Democrats in both the House of Representatives and the Senate, the legislation's future was clouded. With Johnson's ascendancy to power, the political dynamics changed.

George Ready, Johnson's close friend and advisor, later said that Johnson's feelings about race and equality had been underestimated. "Mr. Johnson is one of the least prejudiced or biased or intolerant or bigoted men I have ever met," Ready said. "He has many shortcomings and many failings, but I don't believe there is any racial prejudice in him whatsoever; and this is the thing that became very apparent to most of the Negro leaders when they had a chance to know him personally."[4]

As majority leader of the Senate, Johnson had worked feverishly on the Civil Rights Bill of 1957, a much less defining piece of legislation than was now under consideration. But Bobby Baker, an aide to Johnson at that time, said later, "I can see him now grasping hands and poking chests and grabbing lapels, saying to the southern politicians something like, 'We got a chance to show the way. We got a chance to get the racial monkey off the South's back. We got a chance to show the Yankees that we're good and decent and civilized down here, not a bunch of barefoot, tobacco-chewin' crazies.'"[5]

On November 27, in the chamber of the U.S. House of Representatives, Johnson addressed a joint session of Congress and the American people. Speaking in a soft, quiet voice, acknowledging the grief of the nation, he said that he would "gladly not be standing here today." To honor the fallen president, Johnson said, it would be his intention to carry on his work. Part of that work would be the passage of the civil rights bill. "No memorial oration or eulogy could more eloquently honor President Kennedy's memory," said Johnson, "than the earliest possible passage of the civil rights bill for which he fought so long. We have talked long enough in this country about equal rights. We have talked for one hundred years or more. It is time now to write the next chapter, and to write it in the books of law."[6]

On Thanksgiving Day, King preached a sermon. Afterward, speaking to a graduate student at the University of Wisconsin named Donald Smith, King suggested that Kennedy's death, ironically, might improve chances for civil rights gains. "It may well be," King said, "that the president's death will speed this up. Because I'm convinced that, had he lived, there would have been continual delays and attempts to evade it at every point and water it down at every point. But I think his memory ... will cause many people to see the necessity for working passionately and unrelentingly to get this legislation approved."[7]

King and Johnson first met at the White House on December 3, 1963. As he first stepped into the Oval Office, the five-foot seven inch King was immediately struck by the physical size of the president. He had heard stories of the intimidating presence of Johnson and now he saw it firsthand. Before the meeting, Clarence Jones, one of King's advisors, told King to stress their common southern roots, everything from food to religion to speech. King, said Jones, had much more in common with Lyndon Johnson than he did with John F. Kennedy.

Jones was correct. The two chatted amiably and then quickly talked strategy. The task of getting the bill through Congress, Johnson said, would be a tall one. It would take intensive lobbying, finding common ground, and applying pressure tactics at the right time. Johnson advised King to work with his organization on voter registration and congressional lobbying and to refrain from large public demonstrations while the legislation was pending in Congress. King made no promises regarding tactics but issued a very positive statement to waiting reporters after leaving the Oval Office. "I was very impressed by the president's energy and determination," King said. "As a southerner, I am happy to know that a fellow southerner is in the White House who is concerned about civil rights."[8]

In early 1964, King set out on an exhausting trip to raise money for the cause and to impress on supporters the need to contact their representatives on the civil rights bill. He shuttled across the country, speaking in San Francisco, Milwaukee, and Honolulu and cashing in for the SCLC on the national prominence that the March on Washington had afforded him. By the end of January, it was clear that passage of the bill was fairly certain in the House of Representatives but seriously endangered in the Senate by a threatened filibuster.

The key to Senate passage of the civil rights bill was minority leader Everett Dirksen of Illinois. Only with substantial votes from Senate Republicans could the bill's supporters hope to overcome southern Democratic opposition. The critical role to help the president convince Dirksen and other Republicans to support the legislation fell on the shoulders of Vice-President Hubert Humphrey of Minnesota, a long-time civil rights advocate.

Humphrey recalled Johnson's directions: "The bill can't pass unless you get Ev Dirksen. You and I are going to get Ev. It's going to take time. We're going to get him.... You get in there to see Dirksen. You drink with Dirksen! You talk with Dirksen! You listen to Dirksen."[9]

Humphrey worked tirelessly to convince Dirksen and others. Nevertheless, the road to passage was rocky as opponents filibustered it in the Senate for three months. In past filibusters on civil rights, the southern senators, under the leadership of Georgia Democrat Richard Russell, had with superior discipline worn down their opponents until they agreed to a compromise. This time things would be different. In the end, a coalition of moderate northern Democrats largely from the Northeast and Republicans led by Senator Dirksen would steer its passage.

Meanwhile, King had decided not to take the president's advice about demonstrations. The action was in St. Augustine, Florida, and he was headed there to join it.

ST. AUGUSTINE

Founded in 1565 by the Spanish, St. Augustine, Florida, is the oldest city in the United States. In 1964 it was one of the most segregated cities in the country, a haven for the KKK. Despite the threats and intimidation of the Klan, St. Augustine had a number of civil rights advocates, especially Robert Hayling, a dentist prominent in the black community. On one occasion, Klan members fired a volley of rifle shots into the Hayling home, barely missing his wife and killing his dog.

Later, Hayling and three other civil rights proponents were kidnapped, beaten, and left semiconscious, stacked like firewood. If not for the misgivings of one of the whites who had been along, the four men would have undoubtedly been burned alive. As it was, Hayling was hospitalized for 14 days, suffering several broken bones and a crushed mouth. The attackers were never brought to justice. The City Council not only refused to do anything to stop the KKK; it refused even to speak to civil rights workers about desegregating restaurants or hotels or hiring blacks for city jobs.

In 1963, Hayling, unbowed by his brush with death, organized campaigns against local segregated public facilities catering to tourists. Lacking numbers of people and dollars and unable to get national attention, Hayling appealed to King for help.

The principal black community in St. Augustine, Lincolnville, was established at the end of the Civil War and was home to freed slaves. For a time the 100-square-block area was called "Little Africa," and later, the "Harlem of the South." In the spring and summer of 1964, Lincolnville was the epicenter of civil rights demonstrations.

The SCLC called on New England universities to send volunteers to the city and asked Lincolnville residents to provide food and lodging. By the end of one week of protests, police had arrested hundreds of demonstrators, including a delegation of rabbis.

A contingent of three prominent elderly women came from New England, recruited by SCLC leaders. When they tried to enter morning services at Trinity Episcopal Church with a group of black citizens, they faced locked doors and a lecture by church officials. When one vestryman complained about the "do-gooders" from out of state, one of the septuagenarians, Mrs. Malcolm Peabody, mother of Massachusetts governor Endicott Peabody, responded to the "do-gooder" charge with this retort: "That's exactly what we are—or hope we are." Mrs. Peabody later faced arrest by St. Augustine's sheriff as she attempted to have lunch, along with black individuals, at the Ponce de Leon Motor Lodge. The pictures of this grandmother of seven and mother of a state governor, dressed in a pink suit with a pearl necklace, being whisked off to jail, made the pages of national newspapers. But this was only the beginning for St. Augustine.[10]

In early June, King arrived. When told at a sit-in at Monson's Motor Lodge that the restaurant did not serve blacks, King said that he and his friends would wait until it did. On June 11, King and other members of the SCLC were arrested and, like Mrs. Peabody, hauled off to jail.

On June 18, 1964, the manager at Monson's also managed to attract national attention. When he noticed blacks jumping in the motel swimming pool, he threw muriatic acid into the water, drained the pool, and stationed guards around it. The resulting photographs quickly made the wires around the world and became yet additional ammunition in the war of images being waged by King and his lieutenants. One of the photos was even picked up by *Izvestia*, the influential Soviet newspaper.

St. Augustine's combination of white militants and a police force aligned with their interests rivaled Bull Connor's forces in Birmingham. St. Augustine had its own Bull Connor—Sheriff L. O. (Look Out!) Davis, a gentleman who openly cavorted with Klan regulars such as Holstead "Hoss" Manucy, a pig farmer and sometime bootlegger. The police and vigilantes of St. Augustine daily patrolled the streets brandishing shotguns and deer rifles and some holding onto the leashes of German shepherds. For several days, the streets were lined with onlookers waving little Confederate flags as they awaited the melee of the moment. There were clashes at the beach, where black protestors tried to swim. There were clashes every evening near the Old Slave Market on the town square where civil rights marchers and the Klan held opposing rallies. At one point, a Justice Department official wired Attorney General Robert Kennedy in Washington that the streets had become so riotous that there was no chance of early mediation.

Even though Florida's governor finally dispatched state troopers to bring some semblance of law and order, the clashes continued. Andrew Young, one of King's closest advisors, was among about 200 marchers who were attacked by over 500 whites on one occasion. "As I was talking to one man, looking to my left," Young later remembered, "another guy slipped up behind me from the right and slugged me in the jaw. Then someone hit me in the head from the rear with a blackjack, and I don't remember anything after that. Network television cameras were filming, and when I watched what happened on film years later, I saw that when I fell to the ground, I instinctively tried to curl up as we had been taught to do, and then someone kicked and stomped me while I was on the ground. The fact that I grabbed my head probably saved me from serious injury."[11]

Faced with this total street chaos and wild desperation, King managed to persuade most of the battered marchers to retreat into the church, where Ralph Abernathy helped them reach a relative calm. A number of the young blacks had been on the verge of heading home for their guns. Had they done so, St. Augustine would have gone down as the most violent racial battle in King's nonviolent movement. Later, enveloped by near total weariness, King in a low voice said to some friends, "Yes, when things happen like this tonight, you question sometimes, 'What are we doing to these people?'"[12]

The climax of the St. Augustine struggle came as the U.S. Congress in Washington reached an end to its negotiations over the civil rights bill. In St. Augustine, a federal judge imposed orders on the business community to begin desegregation. Negotiations in St. Augustine also led to the appointment of a biracial committee to direct the forward movement of the city toward integration. Soon after the committee was formed, all of its white members resigned. Change would be slow in coming.

On the legislative front, President Johnson's uncanny ability to put together coalitions within the Congress proved to be a mighty sword in the civil rights struggle. With concerted efforts by Attorney General Robert Kennedy and Vice President Humphrey and with the cooperation of Senator Dirksen, the Congress passed the legislation. On July 2, 1964, Johnson gathered supporters in the East Room of the White House to put his signature to the historic legislation. King, along with other civil rights leaders such as Roy Wilkins, James Farmer, Whitney Young, and A. Philip Randolph, came forward to shake Johnson's hand.

The impact of the 1964 act was profound. The most immediate effect was to outlaw discrimination in hotels, restaurants, theaters, and other public accommodations. But the law had a far broader reach, barring employment discrimination on the basis of "race, color, religion, sex or national origin" and ending federal funding for discriminatory programs. For black workers, the act was a legal springboard to allow them employment in textile mills, factories, and other workplaces in the South historically closed to them.

John Lewis, veteran civil rights activist, when later asked about the effects of the 1964 law, said, "Come and walk in my shoes." Recalling the indignity of being unable to try on clothing in department stores and being unable to sit at drugstore lunch counters and of seeing the ever present signs barring access to various facilities including drinking fountains and restrooms, Lewis said, "Those signs are gone, the fear is gone. America is a better nation and we are a better people because of the Act."[13]

But Johnson's indefatigable efforts to pass the bill had other effects. Bill Moyers, a former aide to LBJ, recalled in a statement during a 1990 symposium at the Johnson Library: "The night that the Civil Rights Act of 1964 was passed, I found him in the bedroom, exceedingly depressed. The headline of the bulldog edition of the *Washington Post* said, "Johnson Signs Civil Rights Act." The airwaves were full of discussions about how unprecedented this was and historic, and yet he was depressed. I asked him why. He said, 'I think we've just delivered the South to the Republican Party for the rest of my life, and yours.' "[14]

MISSISSIPPI

There would be no rest for King from the civil rights struggles in the summer of 1964. The flashpoint was now Mississippi.

They called it "Freedom Summer," a campaign in the Deep South to register blacks to vote. Thousands of civil rights activists, many of them white college students from the North, descended on Mississippi and other Southern states to try to end the long-time political disenfranchisement of blacks. Throughout the South, local and state officials systematically kept blacks from voting through formal methods, such as poll taxes and literacy tests, and through more violent methods of fear and intimidation, including beatings and lynchings.

Organizers of Freedom Summer had chosen to focus their efforts on Mississippi because of the state's particularly dismal voting-rights record: in 1962 only 6.7 percent of blacks in the state were registered to vote, the lowest percentage in the country.

By mobilizing volunteer white college students from the North to join them, the coalition scored a major public relations coup, as hundreds of reporters came to Mississippi from around the country to cover the voter-registration campaign. The campaign also organized the Mississippi Freedom Party (MFDP) which later elected a slate of 68 delegates to the Democratic National Convention, held that year in Atlantic City, including Fannie Lou Hamer, who made a dramatic appeal for support from the convention floor.

Freedom Summer activists faced a barrage of threats and harassment throughout the campaign, not only from white supremacist groups, but from local residents and police. Over 30 black churches and 30 black homes were firebombed and more than 1,000 black and white protestors were arrested.

Three of the young civil rights workers, while setting out to investigate a church bombing, were arrested and held in jail for several hours on traffic violations. Following their release from jail, they disappeared. James Chaney, a black volunteer, and two white friends, Andrew Goodman and

Michael Schwerner, were found murdered under a nearby dam six weeks later.

In late July King traveled to Mississippi amidst all sorts of rumors of assassination plots and death threats. In Philadelphia, Mississippi, where the three civil rights workers had been abducted, King stood on a bench at a black community center and said, "Three young men came here to help set you free.... I know what you have suffered in this state—lynchings and murders. But things are going to get better. Walk together, children, and don't you get weary."[15]

Mississippi's Freedom Summer had been long and violent. But later, Fannie Lou Hamer said, "Before the 1964 project there were people that wanted change, but they hadn't dared to come out. After 1964 people began moving. To me it's one of the greatest things that ever happened in Mississippi."[16]

OSLO AND THE NOBEL PRIZE

In October 1964, King entered a hospital in Atlanta, suffering from extreme fatigue. Almost continually on the move, facing down serious threats on his life, continuously watched by the FBI as a suspicious communist sympathizer, taking on the central role in the country's most contentious social issue, making speech after speech, answering a continuous stream of questions from the media, King desperately needed rest.

He was at the same time one of the most admired and despised public figures in American life. Earlier in 1964, he became the first black American to be named *Time* magazine's "Man of the Year." Yet, J. Edgar Hoover insisted he was one of the country's most wretched demagogues. Millions of whites across the country, especially in the South, scorned the man who had caused disruption in the social order.

And now, while in the hospital, King picked up the telephone to take a call from Coretta, who had exciting news that he had been awarded the Nobel Peace Prize of 1964. At the age of 35, he was the youngest recipient in the history of the Nobel Prize, an international award first given in 1901. He was only the third black.

Reflecting King's controversial image, letters of praise and ridicule flooded the offices of the Nobel Prize Committee. One letter was from Eugene "Bull" Connor, still snorting over the Birmingham battle. To select King, said Connor, they were "scraping the bottom of the barrel."[17]

On the other side, A. Philip Randolph sent a congratulatory telegram, telling King that he "richly deserved" the prize "as one of the great prophets and moral leaders of the world." Randolph added, "Your life and leadership not only reflect great credit and honor upon yourself and the Negro race but [are] also an inspiration to Negro youth of this and future generations." He hailed King for his "brilliant and matchless leadership" and bade him "forward in the battle for racial and social justice for black and white Americans."[18]

In November King met with his aides to plan for a major voting-rights campaign in 1965. The target would be Selma, Alabama. He spent some warm time with his family, something that, in the midst of his frenetic pace, he saw as a privilege. In talking with Coretta and his children, he saw a time ahead in his life when this nearly surreal existence would cease, when he could perhaps settle into a relatively quiet job of teaching theology at a college or university.

On December 4, 1964, he and 25 friends and family left the United States for Norway and the Nobel ceremonies. They stopped in London where the party was treated nearly like royalty. At Westminster Palace he met the lord chancellor of Britain and members of Parliament and did not fail to call for economic sanctions against South Africa. From the pulpit of St. Paul's Cathedral, he addressed a congregation of 4,000, giving a sermon called "The Three Dimensions of a Complete Life," the first sermon he had delivered in his ministry at Dexter Church. The group visited Westminster Abbey and the Tower of London and then down Whitehall, past the rows of government buildings. He noted to his traveling companions that the grandeur of London had been built on the backs of African and Indian laborers.

Four days later the plane touched down in Oslo. On December 10, 1964, Martin Luther King, Jr. received the Nobel Peace Prize. For nearly 45 minutes, in a jammed Festival Hall, he sat stiffly, occasionally glancing at Coretta. The orchestra played Gershwin and Mozart in his honor. As King Olav V of Norway and other government officials applauded vigorously, King stepped on stage to deliver his acceptance speech.

Outside Festival Hall, hundreds of torch-carrying students gathered around a giant Christmas tree in the university square and shouted "Freedom Now!" and "We Shall Overcome!"

With references to snarling dogs and fire hoses and the indignities against which the movement had fought, King said "I am mindful that only yesterday in Philadelphia, Mississippi, young people seeking to secure the right to vote were brutalized and murdered." He accepted the award on behalf of the civil rights movement, for the thousands of men, women, and children who had put their lives on the line on behalf of a cause larger than themselves. "I accept the Nobel Prize for Peace at a moment when twenty-two million Negroes of the United States of America are engaged in a creative battle to end the long night of racial injustice. I accept this award in behalf of a civil rights movement which is moving with determination and a majestic scorn for risk and danger to establish a reign of freedom and a rule of justice.... I have the audacity to believe that peoples everywhere can have three meals a day for their bodies, education and culture for their minds, and dignity, equality and freedom for their spirits. I believe that what self-centered men have torn down, men other-centered can build up. I still believe that one day mankind will bow before the altars of God and be crowned triumphant over war and bloodshed, and nonviolent redemptive goodwill will proclaim the rule of the land."[19]

NOTES

1. Coretta Scott King, *My Life with Martin Luther King, Jr.* (New York: Holt Rinehart and Winston, 1969), p. 244.

2. *New York Times*, November 24, 1963.

3. Nick Kotz, *Judgment Days: Lyndon Baines Johnson, Martin Luther King, Jr. and the Laws That Changed America* (Boston: Houghton Mifflin, 2005), p. 16.

4. Jonathan Rosenberg and Zachary Karabel, *Kennedy, Johnson, and the Quest for Justice: The Civil Rights Tapes* (New York: W. W. Norton, 2003), p. 197.

5. Robert A. Caro, *Master of the Senate* (New York: Alfred A. Knopf, 2002), p. 959.

6. Ted Gittinger and Allen Fisher, "LBJ Champions the Civil Rights Act of 1964," http://www.archives.gov/publications/prologue/2004/summer/civil-rights-act-1.html.

7. Kotz, p. 20.

8. Kotz, pp. 66–67.

9. Rosenberg and Karabell, p. 255.

10. Kotz, p. 126.

11. Andrew Young, *An Easy Burden* (New York: HarperCollins, 1996), p. 292.

12. Marshall Frady, *Martin Luther King, Jr.* (New York: Penguin, 2002), p. 142.

13. Michelle Mittelstadt, "40 Years Ago Stroke of Pen Began to Bar Discrimination, July 2, 2004," http://www.civilrights.org/campaigns/brown/details.cfm?id=23865.

14. Gittinger and Fisher.

15. Kotz, p. 180.

16. "Freedom Summer: Three CORE Members Murdered in Mississippi," http://www.core-online.org/history/freedom_summer.htm.

17. Stephen B. Oates, *Let the Trumpets Sound: The Life of Martin Luther King, Jr.* (New York: New American Library, 1982), p. 304.

18. A. Philip Randolph to Martin Luther King, October 14, 1964, A. Philip Randolph Papers, Box 2, Manuscript Division, Library of Congress.

19. "Martin Luther King's Nobel Prize Acceptance Speech," http://www.nobelprizes.com/nobel/peace/MLK-nobel.html.

Chapter 10

SELMA

In 1964, the town of Selma, Alabama, had a population of about 30,000 people. Very few of those voters were black. Of Selma's 15,000 black adults, only 335 were eligible to vote. Poll taxes, literary tests, and other methods of intimidation had done their work well for the white establishment.

A grassroots effort to register black citizens was launched by the Dallas County Voters League in late 1964 with the help of the Student Nonviolent Coordinating Committee (SNCC). When Sheriff Jim Clark and his deputies began openly turning away black applicants at the courthouse, the Voters League appealed to King for help.

In January 1965, King arrived in Selma. As he signed the guest register at the Hotel Albert, a young white man named James Robinson confronted King in the lobby, twice hit him in the head, and kicked him in the groin. King's supporters pulled Robinson off and called the police. Robinson, a member of the States' Rights Party, a neo-Nazi organization, was taken away. Although shaken, King was not seriously injured. It was, nevertheless, an appropriate welcome to King from Selma, Alabama.

Although President Johnson had a year earlier discouraged King from public demonstrations while he lobbied Congress for the civil rights bill, the president now took a completely different approach as he prepared to push through Congress a voting rights bill. He now saw the need to rouse the nation through publicity, and to bring to those millions of television sets across the country the truth about how American blacks had been prevented from their basic right.

He called King in Selma on January 15. "If you can find the worst condition of being denied the right to cast a vote," Johnson said, "and if you just take that one illustration and get it on radio and get it on television, and get it in the pulpits, get it in the meetings, get it every place you can, pretty soon, the fellow that didn't do anything but drive a tractor will say, 'That's not right. That's not fair.' And then that will help us on what we are going to shove through in the end.... And if we do that ... it will be the greatest breakthrough of anything.... The greatest achievement of my administration.... So that's what we've got to do now. And you get in there and help us.[1]

King was already at work filling Johnson's request. In January 1965, he mobilized a series of demonstrations. "We must be willing to go to jail by the thousands," he declared from the pulpit of the Brown Chapel African Methodist Episcopal Church. "We are not on our knees begging for the ballot, we are demanding the ballot."[2]

As orderly groups of black citizens lined up at the courthouse in Selma to register to vote, many were beaten and arrested. But they kept coming, filling the jail cells just as they had done in other campaigns orchestrated by King. With each day's news from Selma, national reporters and television networks focused more and more attention. Inevitably, tensions increased and so did the violence meted out by frustrated and enraged whites.

Dallas County Sheriff Jim Clark, a tough-talking, head-cracking Deep South lawman, had a history with civil rights demonstrators. A year earlier, he had turned his volunteer posse, known mostly for busting up labor organizers, on a group of civil rights marchers. Clark had earned his way into the Bull Connor club of militant lawmen. He was thus a perfect foil for King's nonviolent protest tactics. He would, in other words, act predictably and violently.

By early February more than 3,000 black protesters in Selma had spent time in jail, including hundreds of schoolchildren. Annie Lee Cooper, a 53-year-old woman who helped manage a motel, defiantly stood up to Sheriff Clark, bedecked as usual in his tight-fitting uniform and green combat helmet decorated with the image of the Confederate flag, on the steps of the Dallas County Courthouse. "Ain't nobody scared around here," she told Clark, who then nearly knocked her over with a hard push. Cooper retaliated, throwing three punches to Clark's head that put him on the ground. Quickly, deputies pinned her and Clark whipped out his billy club and began slugging. "Clark whacked her so hard," said John Lewis, "we could hear the sound several rows back."[3]

On February 1, 1965, King gathered with supporters at Brown Chapel for a march to the Dallas County Courthouse nine blocks away. John Rowan, one of the young men there that day, had just graduated from the University of Colorado and had never seen the inside of a jail cell. This day, he, along with the others, realized that they were there to provoke arrest.

After a mass meeting at the church, after the preaching and praying and singing, the group stepped off toward the courthouse into the waiting custody of the police. At the jail, the marchers were herded into a large room. King, along with Abernathy, was the last to enter.

Rowan remembered the scene as the marchers glimpsed the leaders: "We greeted Dr. King with applause, expecting something like a resumption of the mass meeting at Brown Chapel. But Dr. King told us that he was feeling hoarse and would rather not preach, and he suggested we hold a "Quaker-type" meeting instead.... The spirit not only moved some of us to preach that afternoon; it also moved us to sing, both freedom songs I knew and gospel hymns I didn't. Being in jail lent a special intensity to our voices, and those of us pressed up against the walls soon found that if we slapped them in rhythm, they resounded like muffled calypso drums. When enough of us did it, the whole floor began to vibrate. Through the walls we soon heard an answering chorus from the other end of the third floor, where the women were being held. How I wish someone had recorded us that day."[4]

On February 9, King traveled to Washington to meet with President Johnson about the developing events in Selma. Johnson told King that he was now preparing to send to the Congress voting-rights legislation and once again told King that the pressure of the demonstrations would help. He told King that he hoped there would be little or no violence.

Sheriff Clark soon answered Johnson's hopes for no violence. When a group of about 200 children and teenage demonstrators arrived at the courthouse, Clark had a new experience in mind for them. Clark and his men led them on a forced march. Off through the countryside the police herded the young people at a faster and faster pace, leaving some vomiting from exhaustion. Now, faced with this example of police overreaction, many white citizens realized that the situation in Selma was careening out of control. Some called for Clark to reign in some of the police action.

On February 18, protesters carried out a night march from Selma to nearby Marion, Alabama to protest the arrest of one of the SCLC field secretaries, James Orange. Police and state troopers attacked. A 26-year-old man named Jimmie Lee Jackson was shot to death while trying to protect his mother from being pummeled inside a cafe during the melee. One observer called it "one of the most vicious situations that was in the whole Civil Rights Movement.... They beat people at random. They didn't have to be marching. All you had to do was be black. And they hospitalized probably fifteen or twenty folks. And they just was intending to kill somebody as an example, and they did kill Jimmie Jackson."[5]

Orange said that the protesters should carry Jackson's casket all the way to Governor Wallace in Montgomery. Many SCLC members believe that it was Orange's comment that helped convince the leadership to plan a march on Montgomery. It was at Jackson's memorial service on February 26, 1965, that King announced that such a march would begin on Sunday, March 7. King declared: "We will be going there to tell Governor Wallace that we aren't going to take it anymore!"[6]

As the televised images of billy-club fury startled television viewers, hundreds decided to make the trek to Alabama to lend their own voices of protests. They included 450 white clergymen, nuns, and rabbis.

On March 7, 1965, some 600 civil rights demonstrators marched east out of Selma, Alabama on U.S. Route 80 toward Montgomery, the state capitol, to petition Governor George Wallace for the right of black Alabamans to vote. The day would become known in civil rights history as "Bloody Sunday."

After speaking with President Johnson, King had attempted to delay the march for a day. Local civil rights leaders argued that the marchers were ready to go and did not want to delay. Joined by Jim Bevel, Andrew Young, and Hosea Williams, they headed for the Edmund Pettus Bridge six blocks away.

At the bridge were state troopers and scores of Sheriff Clark's posse, armed with bullwhips, clubs, and even lengths of rubber tubing wrapped in barbed wire. Alabama state trooper Major John Cloud loudly proclaimed through a bullhorn that the assembly was unlawful and that "It would be detrimental to your safety" to continue it. Cloud told them they had two minutes to comply but seconds later his troopers charged. With tear gas grenades popping and gas-masked officers pounding marchers with nightsticks, the assault began.[7]

The bridge was soon a cauldron of flailing whips in the fog of teargas and cattle prods in use at a place where there was no cattle. For the posse, it was terror time. They beat and gassed the marchers. One member of the posse followed a young black boy and hurled him through a stained-glass window of nearby First Baptist Church. Cheers erupted from groups of white onlookers assembled alongside the road.

Joanne Bland, who was 11 years old, was on the bridge that day. Looking forward to a day of marching and singing, she was engulfed, like the others, in pandemonium. "People were screaming, running." A horse galloped over a woman, Bland said. "I will never forget that sound."[8]

Clark's work would soon be international news. That night, television stations interrupted their coverage to show clips of the violence from Selma. Ironically, ABC was showing a documentary on Nazi war crimes. One viewer remembered his feelings upon seeing the clash between the marchers and the police: "A shrill cry of terror, unlike any that had passed through a TV set, rose up as the troopers lumbered forward, stumbling sometimes on the fallen bodies.... Periodically the top of a helmeted head emerged from the cloud, followed by a club on the upswing. The club and the head would disappear into the cloud of gas and another club would bob up and down. *Unhuman*. No other word can describe the motions.... My wife, sobbing, turned and walked away, saying, 'I can't look any more....'"[9]

There on the evening news, and the next week in magazines, was the sight of marcher Amelia Boynton, clubbed unconscious, draped over the highway median, while troopers adjusted their riot gear, fondled their night sticks, and awaited further orders. A long-time civil rights activist whose real estate office doubled as SNCC headquarters, Amelia Boynton had been a specific target.

King, who had been preaching in Atlanta on "Bloody Sunday," immediately started making plans for a new march on Tuesday. He called on people from all over the country to join him in Selma, especially religious leaders. Shocked by what they had seen on television, hundreds of people, many of them influential clergymen, decided to change whatever plans they had and to head to Selma.

Across the nation, the televised images from Alabama rocked the nation. Sitting in living rooms all over America, viewers could see black demonstrators attempting to protest peacefully being attacked by fellow Americans. They could see the racial hate and resentment, built from generations, that was ignited and on full display. It brought to full view the kind of brutality that made the stories about lynchings and murders and the power of the Ku Klux Klan seem more immediate to Americans.

Ironically, as King and his lieutenants plotted the next move in Selma, some civil rights protesters reached Washington. Both the White House and Justice Department were targets of sit-ins by activists calling for increased federal action. The sight drove President Johnson slightly apoplectic. This administration had done more for black citizens as any in American history, he fumed, and he was planning to do more. The pickets should be in Selma or Montgomery or almost anyplace else besides the White House.

On March 9, King began a second march. This time 15 hundred strong crossed the bridge before meeting up with the troopers on the other side. After King led the marchers in prayer, he asked them to turn back to avoid further violence. They did. King would wait until he had worked out with White House officials better security plans for the marchers before heading to Montgomery.

On March 11, James Reeb, a white Unitarian-Universalist minister from Boston who had arrived to join the march, went to dinner at a black restaurant with two friends, Chuck Olsen and Orloff Miller. Unfamiliar with Selma, they took a wrong turn while heading back to their lodgings. In front of the Silver Moon Café, a hangout for tough whites very much against out-of-state protesters, they were confronted. In the ensuing argument, Reed was bashed in the head with a club. When his friends drove Reed to the tiny Selma hospital, they were advised to take him to the hospital in Birmingham, a two-hour drive. By the time they arrived, Reed, suffering from a massive head fracture, was in grave condition. He died several days later.

Richard Leonard, another of the several white Unitarian-Universalist ministers like Reeb who had come to Selma from the North, was at the memorial service where King delivered the eulogy: "King asked rhetorically, 'Who killed Jim Reeb?' He answered: A few ignorant men. He then asked, 'What killed Jim Reeb?' and answered: An irrelevant church, an indifferent clergy, an irresponsible political system, a corrupt law enforcement hierarchy, a timid federal government, and an uncommitted Negro population. He exhorted us to leave the ivory towers of learning and storm the bastions of segregation and see to it that the work Jim Reeb had started be continued so that the white South might come to terms with its conscience."[10]

On March 15, 1965, President Johnson spoke to a specially convened joint session of Congress, and to millions of television viewers. Johnson, vowing to bring down the last vestiges of legal segregation, embraced the aims of the civil rights movement through the words of the Negro spiritual that had become its anthem.

"At times," Johnson declared, "history and fate meet at a single time in a single place to shape a turning point in man's unending search for freedom. So it was at Lexington and Concord. So it was a century ago at Appomattox. So it was last week in Selma, Alabama…. Wednesday I will send to Congress a law designed to eliminate illegal barriers to the right to vote.... There is no constitutional issue here. The command of the Constitution is plain. There is no moral issue. It is wrong—deadly wrong—to deny any of your fellow Americans the right to vote in this country. There is no issue of States rights or national rights. There is only the struggle for human rights.... But even if we pass this bill, the battle will not be over. What happened in Selma is part of a far larger movement which reaches into every section and State of America. It is the effort of American Negroes to secure for themselves the full blessings of American life. Their cause must be our cause too. Because it is not just Negroes, but really it is all of us, who must overcome the crippling legacy of bigotry and injustice.... And we *shall* overcome."[11]

It was an astonishing speech. The white southerner who had ascended to the presidency through tragedy embraced the civil rights movement on its own terms and in its own language. He made himself part of it. Watching the president's address on television in the living room of a friend's home in Montgomery, King wiped tears from his eyes.

For President Johnson, the Selma struggle had taken on new dimensions after "Bloody Sunday." Johnson decided to use Buford Ellington, the former governor of Tennessee, as an intermediary with Wallace. After a personal meeting with Wallace and with reports about Wallace's reactions to the unfolding crisis from Ellington, Johnson became totally exasperated with Wallace's deception and guile. Johnson told Ellington, "[Y]ou're dealing with a very treacherous guy, and y'all must just not even come in quoting him anymore."[12]

Soon, SCLC successfully petitioned a federal district judge for an order barring police from interfering with another march to Montgomery. U.S. District Judge Frank Johnson not only ordered that the march be allowed to proceed but that Alabama's state and local officials protect the marchers. Shortly after the court acted, President Johnson federalized the Alabama National Guard. For this march, there would be no shortage of protection. The FBI, army helicopters, and U.S. marshals also arrived.

On Sunday, March 21, 14 days after Bloody Sunday, King and more than 3,000 other marchers set out from Brown A.M.E. Church, crossed over the Edmund Pettus Bridge, and this time did not stop until they reached Montgomery. For five days, the road between Selma and Montgomery was lined with marchers. Among those at the head with King were fellow Nobel Peace Prize winner Ralph Bunche and theologian Rabbi Abraham Heschel.

More than 3,000 people, including a core of 300 marchers who would make the entire trip, left Selma accompanied by federal marshals and FBI agents dispatched to Alabama by President Lyndon Johnson. Along

Highway 80, much of it two lanes lined by cotton fields, the marchers walked 12 miles and day and slept in fields. By the time they reached the state capitol on March 25, they numbered about 25,000.

The marchers included many of the heroes of the civil rights movement, such as Rosa Parks and John Lewis. It was a triumphant moment, a return to Montgomery, where the civil rights movement had started 10 years earlier with the Montgomery bus boycott.

As they reached the town square in front of the Alabama state Capitol, the marchers sang out:

Keep your eyes on the prize, hold on, hold on

I've never been to heaven, but I think I'm right.[13]

At the march's end, at the Alabama State Capitol building, King led a delegation that presented a petition to Governor Wallace demanding voting rights for blacks. King talked about the mighty walk for freedom they had just completed, about the spirit and fortitude of those who were part of the movement and how they would never be turned away from their rights, about their resolve even in the face of beatings, and bombings, and rifle fire.

On live television, King addressed a large throng. As she sat listening to the speeches Coretta looked over at Rosa Parks, thinking of the struggle of the last 10 years. From those days of the movement, they had come a long way, desegregating buses, achieving the right to use public accommodations, and making progress toward school integration. Most important, she realized that the movement had gained national prominence and now involved many whites. "When I looked out over the big crowd," she said, "I saw many white people and church people. There were more church people involved than in any demonstration we had ever had, and I said to Martin later that it was perhaps the greatest witness by the church since the days of the early Christians."[14]

King marked the occasion with a defiant call. "We are on the move now," he declared, "Like an idea whose time has come, not even the marching of mighty armies can halt us. We are moving to the land of freedom.... I know you are asking today, 'How long will it take?' Somebody's saying, 'How long will prejudice blind the visions of men?...' I come to say to you this afternoon, however difficult the moment, however frustrating the hour, it will not be long, because truth crushed to earth will rise again. How long? Not long, because no lie can live forever. How long? Not long, because you shall reap what you sow. How long? Not long."[15]

Among those listening to King's speech was Viola Liuzzo, a white mother of five and the wife of a Teamster Union official from Detroit. She traveled to Selma in March of 1965 and served as a volunteer during the Selma to Montgomery march. That night, she was driving back to Montgomery after dropping a load of passengers in Selma. With her was a black teenager, Ben Mouton. Suddenly, four men in another car began chasing the two, pulled alongside the car, and fired several shots. Shot twice in the head, Liuzzo died instantly. Mouton ran the car into a ditch, played dead, and survived. Viola Liuzzo's death was a reminder, King said, that blacks in America were "still in for a season of suffering."[16]

On August 6, 1965, President Johnson signed the Voting Rights Act that he had proposed in his speech of March 15. The law gave to the federal government broad regulatory and enforcement powers to supervise voter registration and elections in counties that had a history of discrimination in voting. It banned the use of literacy or other voter qualification tests that had sometimes been used to prevent blacks from voting. By 1969, 61 percent of voting-age blacks in America were registered to vote, compared to 23 percent in 1964. In Alabama alone the number of registered black voters jumped from 92,700 in 1965 to 250,000 in 1967.

Years later, John Lewis, who was 25 years old at the time of Bloody Sunday and who later became a U.S. Congressman, said that Selma "was a pivotal moment. It was a turning point in the whole struggle for civil rights and the whole struggle for the right to vote. Because some of us gave a little blood on the bridge, it helped to expand our democracy, made it possible for people to come in." The Voting Rights Act was signed in Washington, said Lewis, but its impetus and power came from the "streets of Selma on Highway 80 between Selma and Montgomery."[17]

NOTES

1. American RadioWorks, "The President Calling," http://americanradioworks. publicradio.org/features/prestapes/c1.html.

2. Nick Kotz, *Judgment Days: Lyndon Baines Johnson, Martin Luther King, Jr. and the Laws that Changed America* (Boston: Houghton Mifflin, 2005), p. 254.

3. Chuck Stone, "Selma to Montgomery," *National Geographic* (February 2000), p. 98.

4. John Rowan, "Dr. King's Dinner," *American Heritage* (February 2000), p. 28.

5. Steven Kasher, *The Civil Rights Movement: A Photographic History, 1954–68* (New York: Abbeville Press, 1996), p. 165–66.

6. Kotz, p. 276.

7. Steven Weisenburger, "Bloody Sunday," *Southwest Review* (2005), p. 175.

8. Ellis Cose, "Back on the Bridge," *Newsweek* (August 8, 2005), p.30.

9. Kasher, p. 168.

10. Richard Leonard, "Selma 65: The View from the Balcony," *UU World* (May/June 2001), pp. 23–24.

11. "President Lyndon B. Johnson's Special Message to the Congress: The American Promise," March 15, 1965, http://www.lbjlib.utexas.edu/johnson/ archives.hom/speeches.hom/650315.asp.

12. President Johnson to Buford Ellington, March 18, 1965, 9:13 P.M. Tape WH 6503.10, Citation #7124, Recordings of Telephone Conversations—White House Series, Recordings and Transcripts of Telephone Conversations, Lyndon B. Johnson Library.

13. Kotz, p. 323.

14. Coretta Scott King, *My Life with Martin Luther King, Jr.* (New York: Holt, Rinehart and Winston, 1969), p.268.

15. American RadioWorks.

16. Juan Williams, *Eyes on the Prize: America's Civil Rights Years, 1954–1965* (New York: Viking Penguin, 1987), p. 283.

17. CNN Transcripts, March 7, 2005, http://transcripts.cnn.com/ TRANSCRIPTS/0503/07/ltm.04.html.

Chapter 11

TAKING ON CHICAGO

Shortly after the signing of the Voting Rights Act, King was hopeful that the nonviolent movement toward legal and social equality for blacks would continue to make solid progress. Nevertheless, in August 1965, the Los Angeles neighborhood of Watts exploded in rioting after a traffic incident. The hostility between the black neighborhood and the Los Angeles police, inflamed throughout the summer, erupted into such chaos and violence that over 30 people were killed, almost all of them black. More than 3,500 people were arrested, many for looting stores and setting fire to buildings and automobiles. The clash was of such a magnitude that the National Guard was called out to restore order.

Soon, ghettos in a number of American cities across the country would erupt in rioting. As the civil rights movement directly challenged the existing economic and political power structures, as it demonstrated that reformers could indeed make a difference in the lives of ordinary minority citizens, it inevitably raised expectations and intensified pressures for immediate change. Thousands of black Americans who had been living their lives resigned to the racial caste system that deprived them of basic rights and opportunities now saw the chance for something better. But as increasingly strident demands for change were met with fierce resistance and racial animosity, the delicate stability in many urban centers of America threatened to blow apart.

King was deeply distressed by the racial violence. He decided to press his movement for social and racial justice into the large urban areas of the North. King said, "We've been responsible through the nonviolent movement for giving the downtrodden hope. Not just in the South, but all over the country. People are rioting because their rising expectations, engendered by us, are not fulfilled in the North. So we can't act like we have nothing to do with them, like they aren't our people too just because they live in Chicago."[1]

Although he was concerned that his efforts in northern cities might lead to heated exchanges between protesters and law enforcement and the public, he believed that the civil rights movement must continue to mount pressure for equal treatment and economic independence. King turned his attention to the more basic aspects of life in the ghetto. He was determined to broaden the movement by focusing on issues relating to poverty. His target was now Chicago.

CHALLENGING CHICAGO'S SOCIAL ORDER

On January 26, 1966, King and two aides from SCLC moved into a dingy, four-room apartment on the third floor of 1550 S. Hamlin Avenue in the Lawndale section of Chicago. The apartment was chosen as exemplifying typical ghetto living quarters. King and other civil rights leaders and local officials and ministers planned for marches and boycotts. Their demands were to end discrimination in housing, employment, and schools in Chicago. The campaign would become known as the Chicago Freedom Movement.

When King decided to tackle Chicago, he was challenging one of the foremost political figures in the United States, Mayor Richard J. Daley. Short, stocky, a lifetime resident of Chicago and a veteran of its political wars, Daley had survived battles with mob figures, eager political toughs, labor organizers, and other challengers to reach a position unrivaled by any other mayor of a major American city. Through rigorous and ingenious use of patronage, a network of political operatives at his command, and threats of force and intimidation, Daley, as they said in Chicago, made the trains run, even if he seemed to skirt the law at every turn.

Daley was not about to let a civil rights leader from the South, even a man of King's stature, come into Chicago and tell the mayor how to run his city. Unlike other cities and towns where King and SCLC had conducted campaigns, the local political leaders, at least in Chicago's black wards, were themselves black. They, too, resented King's effrontery in coming to Chicago to make an example to the world of how the color of an individual's skin meant that he was doomed to a ghetto existence.

King did have many black leaders and pastors at his side, such as the Reverend Clay Evans, who welcomed King to his Fellowship Missionary Baptist Church. But others feared repercussions and a disruption of whatever privileges they enjoyed. For example, the Reverend Joseph H. Jackson, pastor of the historic Olivet Baptist Church on Chicago's south side and the president of the National Baptist Convention, the largest African American religious association, was sharply critical of King's plans for Chicago, warning of the inevitable harmful repercussions of civil disobedience. Echoing Jackson's concerns was Ralph Metcalfe, the former Olympic sprinter and a leading black alderman. Black citizens did not need King to campaign in Chicago, said Metcalfe. They were perfectly able to govern themselves.

As for Daley himself, a man who had gone out of his way to praise King's efforts in the South, he responded coyly when told of King's plans. "The presentation of his position against poverty and discrimination, for which he was deservedly awarded the Nobel Peace Prize," Daley said, "is a position that all right-thinking Americans should support."[2]

Early on, Daley, an artist at political gaming, tried a cagey preemptive maneuver. In answer to the questions raised by King and other civil rights leaders about the problems facing poor blacks in Chicago, the mayor proudly and loudly announced his own new program to clean up the city slums by the end of 1967.

Thus, as King came to Chicago, he would be taking on a wily leader with many self-interested followers. The odds for the civil rights leader were not good.

OPERATION BREADBASKET

While preparing for the showdown in Chicago with Mayor Daley and his entrenched political interests, King moved on another economic front. He had admired the success in the early 1960s of the efforts of the civil rights activist Leon Sullivan in Philadelphia, who had launched a program of community self-help and empowerment, based on ideas of nonviolence and direct action. Like King, Sullivan had learned the concepts of Gandhi in his graduate studies. His operation in Philadelphia, called "Selective Patronage," sought to boycott companies that did not offer employment to black men and women. With Sullivan's work as a model, King decided to engage the SCLC in its own efforts at "selective buying campaigns."

King would call the program "Operation Breadbasket." To increase the number of jobs for low-income blacks, the organization's tactic would be to threaten a boycott on businesses that did not cooperate in the program. If the businesses did not comply, the boycotts would go forward. As King said, the logic behind such efforts is "if you respect my dollar, you must respect my person," and that Negroes "will no longer spend our money where we cannot get substantial jobs."[3]

The first successful Breadbasket operation began in Chicago under the direction of a young student at Chicago Theological Society—Jesse Jackson. Passionate, attractive, a stirring speaker, Jackson had shown up during the Selma battles and had impressed a number of King lieutenants and King himself. With a rare combination of energy and dynamism, Jackson threw himself into situations and causes, whether he was invited or not. He was brash, yet enormously effective, and King saw right away his potential to help the movement.

In April 1966, from his office in a small south-side house, Jackson launched the first salvo in Operation Breadbasket's campaign to bring greater economic and consumer power to the black community. The first target was a dairy that serviced over 100 outlets in the black areas of Chicago. After Jackson's request to examine the employment rolls of the company was rejected, a team of pastors from black churches asked their parishioners to boycott the company's products. Within a few days, the company offered a resolution: they would add 44 jobs, or 20 percent of their job force, to black ghetto residents.

"Our tactics are not ones of terror," Jackson asserted. "Our biggest concern is to develop a relationship so that the company has a respect for the consumer and the consumer will have respect for the company." As buying power increased for members of the black community, he said, "they will be able to spend more money. So it benefits both sides."[4]

Jackson said that blacks must be able to control the basic resources of the communities in which they lived. "We want to control the banks, the trades, the building construction and the education of our children. This desire on our part is a defensive strategy evolved in order to stop whites from controlling our community and removing the profits and income that belong to black people. Our programs are dictated by the private-enterprise economy in which we find ourselves."[5]

Jackson's first big victory was against A & P, one of the country's largest grocery chains. For over six months, Breadbasket led a boycott of most of the 36 A&P stores in black areas of Chicago. Housewives joined clergymen on the picket lines in front of the various stores. With surprising discipline, the black community stayed away from A & P stores.

Inside the stores, down aisle after aisle, the appearance was eerie, as if the stores were essentially closed. By the time the boycott played itself out, nearly 200 blacks had jobs—from delivery boys to department managers. In addition, the chain agreed to increase its sale of products produced by black businessmen, to use black-owned janitorial and exterminating companies, and to use black-owned banks as business partners in ghetto areas. Jewel Tea Company hired over 600 black workers. Dozens of other companies did not wait for the actual boycotts to begin but notified Jackson that new jobs were opening up for blacks. "You can't calculate the number of jobs made available because they hear those footsteps coming," Jackson told a reporter.[6]

King cited Jackson's work in Chicago for another important gain. It spearheaded the development of black-controlled financial institutions that were sensitive to the problems of poverty in the black communities. As black-run banks acquired greater resources, they in turn could make loans to black businessmen who could hire black workers who would then have greater financial resources of their own to spend. Operation Breadbasket was thus helping to create an economic cycle of production and consumerism within those communities.

Jackson's work in Chicago was so successful that he was asked to expand Operation Breadbasket to other cities. This campaign catapulted Jackson to the forefront of the civil rights movement, and, later, to prominence as a national political leader.

THE MEREDITH MARCH

As on so many other occasions in King's life, careful plans gave way to immediate crises. On June 6, word reached King that civil rights leader James Meredith had been shot in Mississippi.

After serving in the Air Force from 1951 to 1960, Meredith attended Jackson State College for two years. In 1962, he fought successfully to be the first black student to enter the University of Mississippi. Meredith's fight had sparked riots on the Oxford, Mississippi, campus that had cost two lives.

Now, Meredith was on another civil rights journey. He decided to walk from Memphis, Tennessee, to Jackson, Mississippi, to express the fearlessness and determination of blacks in exercising their voting rights. The 32-year-old activist's "March Against Fear" reached Hernando, Mississippi, 30 miles from his starting point. A walking stick in one hand and a Bible in the other, he went no further that day. A man rose from bushes alongside the road and shot Meredith three times in the back and legs. Because he had seen the shooter just before the assassination attempt, Meredith was able to turn and fall to ground. His dive saved his life. FBI agents trailing Meredith along the route apprehended the assailant who was later sentenced to five years in prison.

King immediately flew to Memphis to see Meredith, whose wounds were not serious. The two were soon talking with Stokely Carmichael of the Student Nonviolent Coordinating Committee and Floyd McKissick of the Congress of Racial Equality about resuming the march to Jackson. It now became known as the "Meredith March."

While Meredith recuperated in Memphis, scores of marchers resumed his trek from Hernando. They walked for nearly three weeks and helped to register thousands of black Mississippians to vote. Meredith himself rejoined the march on June 26 as they entered Jackson.

It was during the Meredith March that Stokely Carmichael, after being arrested and posting bond in Greenwood, Mississippi, created a stir in a speech to the marchers. He told them that it was time to demand "Black Power." It was a phrase that would define part of the civil rights movement. It was a phrase inimical to the nonviolent approach preached by Martin Luther King since the beginning of his civil rights movement. King later called Carmichael's phrase "an unfortunate choice of words." They were words that King would be forced to confront and combat in the months and years ahead.[7]

THE CHICAGO CAMPAIGN

On July 10, 1966, at Chicago's mammoth Soldier Field, between 30,000 and 60,000 people, both black and white, attended a rally its organizers called "Freedom Day" in 100 degree heat. Mahalia Jackson sang. And King was able to persuade Archbishop John Cardinal Cody to issue a statement in support of King's work. "Your struggle and your sufferings," the message said, "will be mine until the last vestige of discrimination and injustice is blotted out here in Chicago and throughout America."[8]

Afterward, approximately 5,000 marchers, led by King, paraded from Soldier Field to City Hall where the civil rights leader posted on the door of Mayor Richard J. Daley demands for what he called "The Non-Violent Freedom Fighters." King's demands were to end discrimination in housing, employment, and schools in Chicago.

This action of posting demands on the door of the leader echoed that of King's namesake, Martin Luther, the German theologian, who nailed his 95 theses (statements for debate) on the door of the Castle Church in Wittenberg, Germany, on October 31, 1517. Martin Luther's act launched the Protestant Reformation.

King pointed out to reporters that the 800,000 black citizens in Chicago, tightly segregated in tenement housing, paid inflated rents for substandard buildings; they went to schools ill-equipped to give a quality education; and they suffered an unemployment rate of 13 percent, a figure much higher than the national average. Most could look forward only to unskilled jobs. The cycle of poverty and racism was, he said, abhorrent to what the United States should represent.

As he prepared for the Chicago campaign's marches, King not only conferred with church leaders and politicians but also with members of Chicago's youth gangs –groups such as the Cobras and the Blackstone Rangers. His message was to resist the calls for violence that they would hear in the coming weeks. One of the gang members said during a meeting, "You mean to tell me I'm sitting here with the cat who's been up there talking to the President. He's been up there eating filet mignon steaks, and now he's sitting here eating barbecue just like me."[9]

Roger Wilkins, one of the Justice Department officials sent to Chicago by President Johnson, was present at one of the meetings King conducted with gang leaders. Wilkins later wrote that King "dealt with those kids with a reverence for their humanity, dignity, belief in their importance that he communicated to them, and with the patience of a saint." Wilkins watched in amazement as King's connection to young men who, at this time in their lives, seemed to live for violence. He managed to convince them that rioting would be counterproductive.[10]

On Tuesday, July 12, Chicago sweltered in heat. As they always had done, black children, unable to use the public swimming pools because of segregation, played in the cool water coming from the city's illegally opened fire hydrants. When a few youths stole merchandise from a disabled ice cream truck, the police arrived, retaliated by shutting off the hydrant, and left. Soon, the youths turned the water back on. When the police returned, they faced a barrage of bricks and bottles and escalating chaos. Residents began throwing objects at passing cars and breaking windows in neighborhood stores. Notified of the escalating tensions, King and other civil rights leaders rushed to the area try to intervene in the raucous behavior. The disturbances eased off overnight.

The following morning, the city responded provocatively. Apparently determined to show their authority, city officials sent workers to keep children from turning on the fire hydrants. Several generations of black children had been able to use the fire hydrants during Chicago heat waves. Not surprisingly, this action infuriated black residents. The neighborhood soon became a battleground.

Into the hostile southwest and northwest sides and nearby suburbs, the demonstrators persisted, warding off insults, flying objects, and death threats. But, as one marcher put it, the determination for social justice was great. "We march," one activist noted, "we return home emotionally drained, from some inner reservoirs replenish our strength, and go back." The discipline of the marchers was impressive. Even gang members, who often served as march marshals, remained nonviolent. "I saw their noses being broken and blood flowing from their wounds; and I saw them continue and not retaliate, not one of them, with violence," King later marveled.[11]

SCLC staff member Stoney Cook remembered the raw, violent mobs with many of the people throwing beer bottles. "Andy Young's car that I parked, they pushed that sucker into a lake. They burned cars. Bricks, firecrackers. It was horrible."[12]

By the end of the week, two individuals had been killed, about 80 injured, two policeman shot, and more than 400 arrested, mostly young black teen-agers. The damage to west side businesses and property was excessive and to the owners, heartbreaking. Daley requested mobilization of the National Guard from Governor Otto Kerner in order to quell the riot.

President Johnson was so concerned over the events that he dispatched to Chicago John Doar and Roger Wilkins of the Justice Department. Daley was quick to blame King and the other leaders of the demonstrations for fomenting violence.

Sensing that they needed a sharper, more focused goal for the Chicago campaign, King and the other leaders decided to concentrate almost exclusively on housing segregation, a principal reason behind the ghetto conditions plaguing so many black Chicagoans. Some activists saw the issue as similar to the old lunch-counter demonstrations that had been so successful earlier in the movement. Chicago realtors became, in this view, the northern George Wallaces, as one activist put it, standing "in the doorway of thousands of homes being offered for sale or rent" and preventing "Negroes and other minorities from choosing freely where they may live."[13]

Chicago activists thus began testing real estate firms for discriminatory practices. With their suspicions confirmed about blacks having very few and strictly proscribed areas in which they could purchase homes, they mounted marches into white neighborhoods to protest unfair black exclusion. Many now referred to the demonstrations as the "open housing campaign."

On July 28, they held a demonstration and all-night vigil at a real estate office in Gage Park. The gathering provoked violent reactions by local residents who threw bottles and rocks at the demonstrators and shouted insults. The police attempted to protect blacks, but this only made the white crowd angrier. By the end of the day, the white mob had wrecked approximately 24 cars, and the injured list stood at 30.

Andrew Young was in the middle of the chaos and later referred to it as the march he would most like to forget. "About ten thousand screaming people showed up to harass, curse, and throw debris on us that Sunday, aided and abetted by crazies from the American Nazi Party and similar folk.... Bottles were flying and cherry bombs were going off. We felt like we were walking through a war zone."[14]

On August 5, as King led another march through an area in southwest Chicago, he and other marchers were pelted with stones by an angry crowd. King was startled at the venom and hatred that he saw from the Chicago mobs. That night, physically tired, battered and emotionally spent, King sat on an old couch of a friend's home on Chicago's south side. His head was not seriously cut by a rock that felled him earlier, but his patience was as thin as a reed. "Frankly, I have never seen as much hatred and hostility on the part of so many people," he said slowly. "To my mind those people represent the most tragic expression of man's inhumanity to man."[15]

The August 5 violence stirred many black citizens. Suddenly, large numbers offered to march. Black preachers and alderman now joined a growing chorus demanding change. The hatred and ugliness highlighted by the demonstrations fueled long-time animosities. The power of the white majority, they now believed, could be challenged.

On August 8, Jesse Jackson, coordinator of Operation Breadbasket, announced that protesters would soon march into Cicero, a white suburb bordering Chicago on the west. With a reputation as one of the most racist towns in the North, Cicero was perhaps the most provocative target that the protestors could have selected. Only a few months earlier, four whites beat to death a black teenager there. In 1951, much of Cicero rioted when a black family tried to move into the community. The threat of a march into Cicero at the same time enraged and frightened city leaders. They saw ahead a possible bloodbath.

Meanwhile, movement leaders organized marches in suburban Chicago Heights, Marquette Park, and Cragin. The leadership also set a date of Sunday, August 28, for the march into Cicero.

Over succeeding weeks, as tensions in the city over the continuing protests mounted, the pressures for a settlement heightened, resulting in a series of meetings between city officials, including Mayor Daley, civil rights activists, real estate agents, and business and religious leaders.

The mayor finally called a meeting with King at the world famous Palmer House Hotel for August 26, 1966. King, Daley, and their supporters met for 10 hours to work out an agreement. King and his associates wanted the right of blacks to purchase housing in any neighborhood of their choice, unrestricted by racial barriers. Daley wanted a halt to the demonstrations and the status quo regarding housing. How the two would breach such a chasm was problematic.

When the participants emerged after the meeting, Daley praised the outcome. King was also apparently satisfied, calling the agreement the "most significant program ever conceived to make open housing a reality in a metropolitan area."[16]

In fact, the agreement contained no guarantees, only pledges by its participants. There was no timetable for implementation. The experience of the Chicago Freedom Movement illustrated the difficulties of transplanting the southern struggle to the North. It also demonstrated the extent to which most of white America was unwilling to embrace racial equality when it threatened their own property rights and what they saw as the quality of their neighborhoods.

Although most observers, including many black leaders, thought that the long campaign in Chicago had made little progress in addressing the perplexing problem of open housing, King was convinced that the effort had at least advanced the struggle for freedom. Nevertheless, the experience of the Chicago summer of 1966 left him disillusioned with the reactions of the white population. He kept seeing the taut, hate-filled faces of the lines of whites that cursed and spat and daily threatened his life. He left Chicago with a new despondency about race relations. Opinion polls across the country revealed that 85 percent of Americans now felt that blacks were demanding too much too fast and that over half admitted they would not live next door to a black individual.

After Chicago, King, as never before, could feel those sentiments in his blood.

NOTES

1. Andrew Young, *An Easy Burden: The Civil Rights Movement and the Transformation of America* (New York: HarperCollins, 1996), p. 386.

2. Eugene Kennedy, *Himself: The Life and Times of Mayor Richard J. Daley* (New York: Viking, 1978), p. 193.

3. Michael Eric Dyson, *I May Not Get There with You: The True Martin Luther King, Jr.* (New York: Touchstone, 2000), pp. 81–82.

4. "Black Pocketbook Power," *Time*, March 1, 1968, p. 17.

5. "Jesse Jackson: A Candid Conversation with the Fiery Heir Apparent to Martin Luther King," *Playboy*, November 1969, http://www.geocities.com/heartland/9766/jackson.htm.

6. "Black Pocketbook Power."

7. John Goldman, "Stokely Carmichael, Black Activist, Dies," *Los Angles Times*, November 16, 1998, http://www.interchange.org/kwameture/latimes111698.html.

8. Kennedy, p. 205.

9. Stephen B. Oates, *Let the Trumpets Sound: The Life of Martin Luther King, Jr.* (New York: New American Library, 1982), p. 378.

10. Roger Wilkins, *A Man's Life: An Autobiography* (New York: Simon and Shuster, 1982), pp. 208–9.

11. James Ralph, Jr., "Dr. King and the Chicago Freedom Movement," *American Visions* (August/September 1994), p. 30.

12. Marshall Frady, *Martin Luther King, Jr.* (New York: Penguin Books, 2002), p. 212.

13. Ralph, p. 32.

14. Young, p. 413.

15. Ralph, p. 33.

16. "Housing Pact Set, Dr. King Calls Off Chicago Marches," *New York Times*, August 27, 1966.

Chapter 12

VIETNAM,
BLACK POWER, AND 1967

In the early days of 1967, King faced a turbulent political atmosphere. Because of the soaring costs of the Vietnam War, the Congress and the administration scaled back expansion plans for various antipoverty programs. The fire and spirit of protest among those on the college campuses were now directed far more against the war than on civil rights matters. And the voices that were calling for continued progress in civil rights were now more strident, more spokesmen demanding that change come more quickly and, if necessary, violently. They were the voices of Black Power, which had seemed to rise out the disappointments of the Watts riots and an increasing disaffection of whites toward further concessions in the civil rights struggle.

KING AND THE VIETNAM QUAGMIRE

As did many Americans in positions of power, King felt increasingly disillusioned by the one of the most contentious conflicts in American history—U.S. participation in the Vietnam War. The roots of the country's involvement in the Vietnam struggle reached back to 1954, when communist armies in northern Vietnam under the leadership of Ho Chi Minh ousted the French military, which had governed in southern Vietnam for 100 years. Outnumbered and overpowered, despite some assistance by the U.S. government, the French suffered a catastrophic defeat at Dienbienphu, a military base in northern Vietnam. The end of the 56-day siege signaled the end of French colonial power in

Indochina. The Geneva Peace Accords, ending the French occupation, stipulated that Vietnam would hold national elections in 1956 to unite the country.

Concerned about the inexorable spread of communism, President Eisenhower and the United States helped create the Government of the Republic of Vietnam or South Vietnam under the presidency of Ngo Dinh Diem. The United States thus began to assume a similar role to that of France as overseer of Vietnam. When the new government in the south refused to hold the national elections promised under the Geneva Peace Accords, the Vietnamese communists began a guerilla war against the south.

President Kennedy sent a team to Vietnam to assess conditions. Although the resulting report called for a large-scale assault, the United States, at least at this point, balked, fearful of being dragged more deeply into the morass that had destroyed French troops.

As Lyndon Johnson assumed the presidency in 1963, the Vietnam conflict loomed as the most intractable problem facing the United States. From the day he took office, Johnson faced the haunting specter of Vietnam. As it became increasingly clear to the U.S. defense planners that the South Vietnamese army was not strong enough to prevent a communist victory, Johnson faced pressure from his military to take more aggressive action against North Vietnam. The Joint Chiefs of Staff advised Johnson to send U.S. combat troops to South Vietnam.

On August 2, 1964, the U.S. destroyer, *Maddox*, was apparently fired upon by three North Vietnamese torpedo boats in the Gulf of Tonkin. In retaliation, the *Maddox* fired back and hit all three, one of which sank. The incident gave Johnson the political ammunition he needed to justify an attack on the North Vietnamese. He ordered the bombing of four North Vietnamese torpedo-boat bases and an oil-storage depot, an attack that had been planned three months previously, and then went on television and told the American people that the attacks were underway. The Congress quickly approved Johnson's decision to bomb North Vietnam and passed what has become known as the "Gulf of Tonkin Resolution" authorizing the president to take all necessary measures against the North Vietnamese.

U.S. involvement in the war deepened. Increasing numbers of dead young Americans arrived back in the country in body bags; political division over the war grew more hostile; the scenes of devastation and death began to appear nightly on American television; rhetoric escalated; and the end of the conflict now seemed no closer than the beginning.

In August 1965, during the annual convention of SCLC, King surprised his listeners by publicly expressing exasperation and deepening regret at the country's direction on the war. He appealed to his colleagues to join in a call for negotiations to end the war and an immediate halt to U.S. bombing operations in Vietnam. His sudden public pronouncements did not play well to his audience that day, and they certainly did not play well in the White House.

Fearful of compromising civil rights legislation before Congress, King muted much of his disdain for the war during 1966. But after President Johnson announced plans to divert antipoverty funds to Vietnam in December 1966, King began once again to assert his opposition to what he considered an immoral and ill-advised war effort.

Shortly after the off-year congressional elections in 1966 in which the Democrats suffered dramatic losses, King talked by phone with President Johnson. Because of King's opposition to the war, the relationship between the two had cooled markedly. But the civil rights leader wanted to make a case to Johnson that he should continue to fight for open housing and other goals of the movement, despite the agonies of the war and its tremendous expenditures. When the two talked, Johnson did not hide his private agony over the war. King sensed that he was deeply troubled and frustrated by the Vietnam stalemate. On one side was the military begging for more troops and on the other were the peace protesters. Johnson told King that he was trying to follow a middle road, a road that sometimes had in it the most hazards. King listened to Johnson, told him that he sympathized with his position, and ended the conversation. When a couple of King's aides asked why he had not even talked about civil rights in the conversation, King said. "There is a time to be a prophet and a time to be a pastor," King said. "A good prophet can also be a good preacher." This was to be the last conversation between the two men.[1]

In January 1967, many of those individuals closest to King, including Coretta, urged him to come out more publicly on Vietnam. Bernard Lee, a close friend and associate of King, remembered seeing him flipping through a copy of *Ramparts* magazine while he ate. Suddenly he froze. "He saw a picture of a Vietnamese mother holding her dead baby," recalled Lee, "a baby killed by our military. Then Martin just pushed the plate of food away from him. I looked up and said, 'Doesn't it taste any good?' and he answered, 'Nothing will ever taste any good for me until I do everything I can to end that war.'"[2]

In February, to a group of antiwar senators, he declared that the involvement by the United States in Vietnam had diverted the attention of the government and the public away from the civil rights movement. Although some activists and newspapers supported King's ideas, most were critical. Many of the civil rights leaders began to disassociate themselves from his antiwar stance and argued that merging the civil rights movement with the peace movement would not be productive. King ignored them.

On April 4, 1967, to a crowd of 3,000 people in Riverside Church in New York City, King delivered a speech entitled "Beyond Vietnam." "I come to this magnificent house of worship tonight because my conscience leaves me no other choice," he said. "In the light of such tragic misunderstanding, I deem it of signal importance to try to state clearly, and I trust concisely, why I believe that the path from Dexter Avenue Baptist Church—the church in Montgomery, Alabama, where I began my pastorate—leads clearly to this sanctuary tonight."[3]

It was cruel and outrageous, King said, for the U.S. government to use the most vulnerable and poor in American society to fight and die for a nation that has refused to seat them in the same schools with whites. How could King, the proponent of nonviolence, stand aside as those in the American ghettos, to whom he had preached that guns and Molotov cocktails were not the answer, were dragged halfway around the world to spread violence? For the sake of those young men and of the soul of the United States, he said, he could not be silent.

"Somehow this madness must cease," he declared. "We must stop now. I speak as a child of God and brother to the suffering poor of Vietnam. I speak for those whose land is being laid waste, whose homes are being destroyed, whose culture is being subverted. I speak for the poor of America who are paying the double price of smashed hopes at home, and death and corruption in Vietnam. I speak as a citizen of the world, for the world as it stands aghast at the path we have taken. I speak as one who loves America, to the leaders of our own nation: The great initiative in this war is ours; the initiative to stop it must be ours."[4]

He called for an end to the bombing and a unilateral cease-fire to encourage negotiations. He called for reducing the U.S. military presence in other Southeast Asia countries such as Laos and Thailand. He asked that the United States realistically recognize that North Vietnam had substantial political support in South Vietnam and must play a role in negotiations and in a future Vietnam government. Finally, he called for the U.S. government to remove all troops by a set date.

After the April 4 speech, King participated as a leader in the 1967 Spring Mobilization for Peace that brought together more than 100,000 people. He advised young men to consider registering as conscientious objectors. He called for a ban on the testing of nuclear devices. He supported disarmament. He talked about the destructive outcome of meeting violence with violence. "The bombs in Vietnam explode at home," he said. "They destroy the hopes of possibilities for a decent America.... The security we profess to seek in foreign adventures we will lose in our decaying cities." Meeting violence with violence, he said, was a way of achieving a double defeat—defeat at home and defeat abroad.[5]

King's bold but controversial stance seriously fractured his national support and standing. Among his fellow civil rights leaders, there was consternation and anger that he had wedged the antiwar movement into the civil rights struggle. Roy Wilkins of the NAACP and Whitney Young of the Urban League chastised King. Black Congressman Adam Clayton Powell derided him, calling him Martin Loser King. Jackie Robinson, the Hall of Fame baseball player and long-time civil rights activist, pleaded with King not to weaken the call for racial justice with a political position that was certain to alienate a large percentage of the American people.

Much of the media, including the *New York Times* and the *Washington Post*, attacked King, as did *Life* magazine. Suddenly, the Nobel Prize winner, the spokesman for morality and teacher of human rights, was on the receiving end of attacks from elements of the public that were usually praising his efforts. The war in Vietnam was not going well but most Americans, King found to his consternation, were not ready to change course.

Even King's father was at first not supportive. Later, he came to believe that his son had been right. But through it all, King's college president and mentor, Benjamin Mays, was steadfast. He said, "I do not agree with the leaders who criticized Dr. King on the ground that he should stick to civil rights and not mix civil rights with foreign policy.... I learned long ago," said Mays, "that there are no infallible experts on war."[6]

As 1968 and a presidential election approached, whatever confidence the Johnson administration exuded about the imminent end of the Vietnam War had been dashed. The North Vietnamese forces had launched a withering offensive against the south early in the year. The nightly scenes on television of the devastation of Vietnamese towns, of injured and scarred civilians screaming after napalm attacks, and of the blood-drenched wounded and maimed being helicoptered into battlefield hospitals were leaving a dark imprint on the minds of people across America. The war seemed never-ending, with vague objectives and purpose. More than half a million American soldiers were still in

Vietnam in 1968, four years since American combat troops had landed. Each week about 200 more Americans and thousands of Vietnamese lost their lives. For King, it was deeply shameful and immoral.

BLACK POWER

In the summer of 1967, along with the horrors of Vietnam, King saw his deepest worries about the growing violence surrounding the civil rights movement become front-page headlines. America's ghettos were aflame. Even as victories had mounted in the civil rights campaign against segregation and disfranchisement and had raised hopes in the black communities around the country for progress toward racial equality, the attempts to force economic rights in the north met with a fiery resistance that even King had not foreseen. The sight of rioting black youths in the inner cities fighting with police became a frightening if not uncommon spectacle on American television news. Over 75 cities witnessed especially brutal confrontations in 1967 alone.

In Newark, New Jersey, 26 blacks lost their lives amid the carnage and in Detroit, Michigan, riots took 40 lives and lasted a full week, with the city's black areas ablaze and enveloped by billowing black clouds of smoke. The violence became so intense that President Johnson, acting on the request of the governor of Michigan, ordered 4,700 U.S. paratroopers to the city to restore order.

King condemned the rioting, but his harshest criticism was for the brutal social conditions under which American blacks were forced to live. Those conditions, he believed, were ultimately at the root of the violence. When King had visited Watts in 1965 after the riots, he said that officials in the city should have anticipated them since the unemployment rate and living conditions in Watts were unconscionably bad. Only a forceful national effort to address the economic inequalities in American society, he thought, could provide a lasting solution.

King himself was now under attack by aggressive black leaders who demanded that the movement turn from nonviolence. They called for "Black Power" and urged their oppressed compatriots not to turn their backs on the physical assaults they continually endured but to resist forcefully. Even with the progress that King had already achieved in the civil rights arena, it was becoming increasingly difficult for him to control an explosive social climate of hatred and fear that threatened to unravel many of the advances already gained.

The strident Black Power philosophy had at its core much of the rhetoric and demands of the early black nationalist movement of Marcus

Garvey in the 1920s and, later, the then-current teachings of Malcolm X. It was a philosophy of black pride and sense of community, economic self-reliance, and a willingness to use force to achieve aims. It was a philosophy that rejected compromise with the white power structure. Some black nationalists looked forward to the day when they could create a separate black nation to maintain and promote their black ancestry.

Malcolm X had been particularly harsh in his criticisms of King's nonviolent strategy to achieve civil rights reforms. During a November 1963 address at the Northern Negro Grass Roots Leadership Conference in Detroit, Malcolm derided the notion that African Americans could achieve freedom nonviolently and also the idea that black or white Americans really want integration. King felt that Malcolm's insistence on violent aggression done blacks a disservice.

Another Black Power advocate, Stokely Carmichael, argued that blacks would always be in a dependent relationship as long as whites could determine their identity. "People ought to understand that we were never fighting for the right to integrate, we were fighting against white supremacy. In order to understand white supremacy we must dismiss the fallacious notion that white people can give anybody his freedom. A man is born free. You may enslave a man after he is born free, and that is in fact what this country does. It enslaves blacks after they're born. The only thing white people can do is stop denying black people their freedom ... someone must stand up and start articulating that this country is not God, and that it cannot rule the world.... . We are on the move for our liberation. We're tired of trying to prove things to white people. We are tired of trying to explain to white people that we're not going to hurt them. We are concerned with getting the things we want, the things we have to have to be able to function. The question is, Will white people overcome their racism and allow for that to happen in this country? If not, we have no choice but to say very clearly, 'Move on over, or we're going to move over you.' "[7]

Born in Port-of-Spain, Trinidad in 1941, Carmichael had moved with his family to Harlem and become a naturalized citizen. Educated at Howard University in Washington, D.C., he became active in a number of areas of civil rights activism. In 1961, he joined a Freedom Ride to Jackson, Mississippi, and was involved in the demonstrations in Albany, Georgia and a hospital workers' strike in New York. After graduating in 1964 with a degree in philosophy, Carmichael joined SNCC's staff in the voter registration drive in Mississippi. Increasingly militant in his outlook, he became skeptical about interracial civil rights activities. In 1965, he helped a group of blacks in Alabama who formed an organization that became known as the Black Panther Party. In May 1966, Carmichael was elected chairman of SNCC. This leadership shift marked SNCC's divergence from King's ideals of inclusive, faith-based, nonviolent direct action.

It was the James Meredith March against Fear in Mississippi in June 1966 that brought Carmichael into direct contact with King, whom he personally admired. Carmichael said, "People loved King.... I've seen people in the South climb over each other just to say, 'I touched him! I touched him!' ... They even saw him like God. These were the people we were working with and I had to follow in his footsteps when I went in there. The people didn't know what SNCC was. They just said, 'You one of King's men?' 'Yes. Ma'am, I am.' "[8]

Nevertheless, although Carmichael and King shared a mutual respect and cordiality, on the central issue of their lives, they were philosophical opponents. King held that the root of the Black Power philosophy was in the disillusionment of a suffering people and a surrender to the idea that real progress was hopelessly distant, if not unlikely. Resorting to violence, King insisted, would alienate possible allies, demean those in the struggle, and ultimately jeopardize any hope of progress.

Although King saw Black Power as a positive step in the necessary accumulation of economic and political power, he worried about the implications of black separatism and its willingness to resort to physical violence if necessary.

A FIGHT FOR THE POOR

The nationwide riots, the ascendancy of the Black Power movement, and the continuing escalation of the Vietnam War bore down on the civil rights leader like a great weight. The only response to the troubles that had befallen the country, King told his friends, was to carry on with the work, to fight even harder, to rally together and convince the nation's leadership to follow an agenda for justice.

In November 1967, King and his advisors began to plan for a second phase in the civil rights struggle, one that would turn the movement toward the economic inequalities and poverty plaguing minority communities across the country. The first decade of King's involvement in racial reform politics had centered on gaining legal and constitutional liberties denied to blacks through institutional and social means—from issues surrounding school integration to voting rights to the equal right to public facilities. Now, King believed, was the time to focus on finding ways for minority groups—African Americans, Indians, Puerto Ricans, poor whites—to extricate themselves from a cycle of poverty in which many were hopelessly mired.

On December 4, 1967, King held a press conference in Atlanta announcing that the SCLC planned a "Poor People's Campaign." It would be the most massive, widespread campaign of civil disobedience yet undertaken, he said, one that "will lead waves of the nation's poor and disinherited to Washington, D.C. next spring to demand redress of their grievances by the United States government and to secure at least jobs or income for all. We will go there, we will demand to be heard, and we will stay until America responds. If this means forcible repression of our movement we will confront it, for we have done this before. If this means scorn or ridicule we embrace it, for that is what America's poor now receive."[9]

From cities and counties around the country, SCLC members would gather in separate groups and make their way to Washington to petition the U.S. government for specific reforms. King told his associates that he expected a hostile reception in Washington. Like Mayor Richard J. Daley of Chicago, President Johnson would react coldly to the notion that demonstrators would come to the seat of the national government, engage in overt civil protests, and expect the government to yield to their demands.

Unlike the 1963 March on Washington that had culminated with King's historic speech at the Lincoln Memorial, this would not be a one-day affair, King explained. The estimated 1,500 protesters would not leave Washington but would stay until some governmental action was taken to alleviate poverty and unemployment.

It took a Selma, King said, before the government moved to affirm the fundamental right to vote to black Americans; it took a Birmingham before the government moved to assure the right to all Americans to public accommodations. His call was not just for black Americans, he said, but to all of America's poor—whites, Indians, Mexican Americans, Puerto Ricans, and others. The marchers would come to Washington, he said, to channel into constructive action the frustration and rage that had ignited the cities in riots, to compel the government to come to the aid of those suffering economic deprivation and discrimination. The marchers would seek an "Economic Bill of Rights" guaranteeing employment to the able-bodied, incomes to those unable to work, increased construction of low-income housing, and an end to housing discrimination.

As King had anticipated, reaction from Washington about a poor people's march caused a minor storm of approbation not only from the White House but from both sides of the political spectrum on Capitol

Hill. Nobody in Washington, it seemed, wanted streams of marchers to swarm to the city; most saw possible anarchy, destruction, and chaos. The overreaction by public officials and the press was remarkable. Senator Robert Byrd of West Virginia, for example, whose career had witnessed many storms of controversy and confrontation, saw fit to denounce King as a self-promoter and rabble rouser whose actions would bring bloodshed and looting to the seat of government.

As King's plans for the Poor People's Campaign proceeded, another labor fight involving black workers came to his attention. In Memphis, Tennessee, black sanitation workers had banded together in a strike against the city, forming a union and lobbying for better working conditions and pay.

A tragic incident involving the death of two black workers had precipitated the strike. In Memphis, sanitation workers were not allowed to seek shelter in nearby buildings or even in the cabs of the garbage trucks during rainstorms. They either had to sit inside the rear compartments with the garbage or position themselves under the trucks. During one particularly heavy downpour two men had been crushed by the rear of their truck as they tried to find cover. The incident exposed to public view just one of many grievances surrounding the work, involving everything from lack of safety to miserable pay. The union was a grass-roots effort to gain a mite of economic power and a semblance of respect for those on the lowest rungs of America's economic ladder.

Newly elected mayor Harry Loebe refused to deal with strike leaders and threatened to fire every striker if they failed to return to work. In early February, when only about one-fourth of the city's sanitation trucks were at work, the city began to hire scab labor.

When community civil rights groups and labor leaders contacted the King organization asking for support, King considered intervening. Although a number of his aides, including Andrew Young, feared that a trip to Memphis would seriously interrupt plans for the Poor People's Campaign, King thought that he could not turn his back on the poorest of workers in Memphis.

On March 28, King, flanked by nearly 200 preachers, was once again on the streets in a major American city leading a protest on behalf of economic and racial justice. The marchers were met with police mace, tear gas, and gunfire. A 16- year-old boy fell dead from police gunfire. Nearly 300 marchers were rounded up and jailed for breaking windows and looting stores. About 60 injuries were reported. National Guardsmen moved into the city and martial law was declared. Memphis was in a state of siege.

After returning to Atlanta briefly, King traveled back to Memphis where he planned to work with city leaders and strikers in an effort to resolve the crisis and to prepare for another march on April 5. He checked into an inexpensive, two-story motel just outside the downtown area. When it was first built in the 1920s, it was named the Windsor and was one of the only hotels in downtown Atlanta that housed blacks. It was now called the Lorraine. King unpacked his bags in Room 306.

NOTES

1. Nick Kotz, *Judgment Days: Lyndon Baines Johnson, Martin Luther King, Jr. and the Laws That Changed America* (Boston: Houghton Mifflin, 2005), p. 371.

2. Marshall Frady, *Martin Luther King, Jr.* (New York: Penguin, 2002), p. 185.

3. *"Martin Luther King: Beyond Vietnam—A Time to Break Silence,* delivered 4 April 1967 at a meeting of Clergy and Laity Concerned at Riverside Church in New York City," http://www.americanrhetoric.com/speeches/mlkatimetobreak silence.htm.

4. *"Martin Luther King: Beyond Vietnam."*

5. "The Ethical Foundations of Dr. King's Political Action, Remarks of Charles V. Willie, Charles William Eliot Professor of Education, Emeritus, On the occasion of Martin Luther King Jr. Day, January 21, 2002, The Memorial Church, Harvard University," http://www.news.harvard.edu/gazette/2002/01.17/99-mlkspeech.html.

6. "The Ethical Foundations."

7. "Stokely Carmichael—Black Power," http://www.americanrhetoric.com/speeches/stokelycarmichaelblackpower.html.

8. "Dr. Martin Luther King, Jr. Papers Project: Encyclopedia: Stokely Carmichael," http://www.stanford.edu/group/King/about_king/encyclopedia/carmichael_stokely.html.

9. "Press Conference Announcing the Poor People's Campaign," http://www.stanford.edu/group/King/publications/papers/unpub/671204–003_Announcing_Poor_Peoples_campaign.htm.

Chapter 13

MEMPHIS

On the evening of April 3, 1968, at the Masonic Temple in Memphis, King, facing an injunction by Memphis city officials preventing him from leading another march, delivered an unusual speech—inspiring, defiant, but pensive. He talked about how far these people surrounding him that night had come together in the movement, how overwhelming had been the odds, and how daunting remained the challenges ahead.

He told them to hold together for the cause of social equality, no matter what happened. "We got some difficult days ahead," King told the overflowing crowd, "But it really doesn't matter to me now, because I've been to the mountaintop. I've seen the promised land. I may not get there with you. But I want you to know tonight, that we, as a people, will get to the promised land."

And then, in a remarkably prescient moment, he looked forward: "But it doesn't matter with me now. Because I've been to the mountaintop. And I don't mind. Like anybody, I would like to live a long life. Longevity has its place. But I'm not concerned about that now. I just want to do God's will. And He's allowed me to go up to the mountain. And I've looked over. And I've seen the promised land. I may not get there with you. But I want you to know tonight, that we, as a people, will get to the promised land. And I'm happy, tonight. I'm not worried about anything. I'm not fearing any man. Mine eyes have seen the glory of the coming of the Lord."[1]

Early the following morning, there was good news for King and his associates. The injunction against the march had been lifted. At midday, preparing to leave the Lorraine Motel to meet with march organizers,

King stepped out from his room onto the balcony. King and Jesse Jackson, standing in the parking lot below, exchanged a few remarks.

And then there was the crack of the rifle shot. Hit in the face and neck, King crumpled on the balcony floor. Andrew Young, Reverend Samuel Kyles, and others raced to his side. Ralph Abernathy, his closest friend, cradled him. Blood covered the balcony.

Kyles, pastor of the Monumental Baptist Church in Memphis and long-time civil rights activist, was with King and Abernathy in King's room of the Lorraine for the last hour of King's life. Kyles had helped arrange for the upcoming march and had been working on the sanitation workers strike since the beginning. That evening King was to have had dinner at Kyles's home, along with Jackson.

"About a quarter of 6:00 we walked out onto the balcony," Kyles remembered. "He was greeting people he had not seen. Somebody said, 'It's going to be cold Doc, get your coat.' He didn't go back in the room. He went to the door and said, 'Ralph, get my coat.' Ralph was in the room putting on shaving lotion. Ralph said, 'I'll get your coat.' He went back to the railing of the balcony and was greeting people again. He said something to Jesse Jackson and said something to some other people. We stood together. I said, 'Come on, guys. Let's go.'" Since that day, Kyles reflected on why he happened to be at that place at that time. He concluded that he was there to be a witness. "Martin Luther King, Jr., didn't die in some foolish, untoward way," Kyles said. "He didn't overdose. He wasn't shot by a jealous lover. He died helping garbage workers."[2]

Kyles also pointed out, as did others, that King had mentioned on occasion that he might never reach age 40. When the bullet ended his life that day in Memphis, he was 39.

During a speech at Kansas State University in January 1968, just a few months before his death, King looked back over the civil rights movement with a sense of pride and awe that so many people—thousands in city after city, march after march—had managed to hurdle great psychological and economic barriers to come together in a mass movement for change. The movement had not been simply to gain the right to sit with whites in classrooms or in buses, he said; it was emblematic of a broader sense that a just society might be possible for them after all. They would have to scratch and fight for every gain and, most important, they would have to remain a unified force. But even with the setbacks and disappointments of recent months and years, King still had faith that they would, indeed, overcome.

As King in the last months of his life joined the black sanitation workers under their banner "I Am a Man," he saw their protest as perfectly geared for the kind of national challenge that lay ahead in the

Poor People's Campaign. Here were exploited and class-bound workers fighting for their proper chance in the system. The Memphis strike was not a diversion from King's larger plan, he believed, but a starting place for demonstrating the need for systemic reform, for action to create jobs and income for those trapped in an unfair ghetto of economic limitations.

Memphis sanitation workers did win their strike. King's death forced the segregationist mayor of Memphis to allow a strike settlement, which may have benefited the city's black middle class most of all. As sanitation worker Taylor Rogers pointed out recently, "city hall is full of blacks, even to the mayor," and organized public workers who vote helped to put them there. Blacks with city and county jobs and in clerical positions as well, he says, "wouldn't be in the position they're in now if it had not been for King comin' here and dyin'."[3]

The success of the Memphis strike opened the way to unionization of the working poor in government jobs across the country, a major area in which unions have expanded for the past 30-plus years.

News of the assassination swept many of the nation's towns and cities into a whirl of fire and rage. In more than 125 locations across the country, entire sections of inner cities were engulfed in rioting and arson. A harried President Johnson dispatched military troops and national guardsmen to several cities. By late April, nearly 50 people had perished in the frenzy. The irony and sadness was towering; the death of the man who had preached nonviolence had provoked retaliatory ferocity, against which he had preached all his life.

Finally, the lawlessness subsided, as if the violent pressure within the inner cities had finally, in a futile burst, spent the last of its energy. The nation turned to mourning. There were memorials and rallies. Public facilities closed for a day in honor of King. On April 8, a bereaved Reverend Ralph Abernathy was chosen to succeed King as SCLC president. He led 42,000 silent marchers, including King's widow, Coretta, and other family members in Memphis, to honor King and to support the sanitation workers.

On April 9, at Ebenezer Baptist Church, pastor King and his family, surrounded by many of the nation's political and civil rights leaders, gathered to pay tribute. Thousands stood outside in the streets weeping.

Two Georgia mules pulled King's mahogany coffin on a rickety farm wagon for over three miles through Atlanta's streets to Southview Cemetery. Former Morehouse College president Benjamin Mays, now 70 years old, had a mutual agreement with his former prize student. Whoever survived, Mays said, would deliver the eulogy. Mays, over 30 years King's senior, sadly fulfilled his part of the agreement.

King was "more courageous than those who advocate violence as a way out," Mays told the mourners. "Martin Luther faced the dogs, the police, jail, heavy criticism, and finally death; and he never carried a gun, not even a knife to defend himself. He had only his faith in a just God to rely on…. If physical death was the price he had to pay to rid America of prejudice and injustice," Mays said of King, "nothing could be more redemptive."[4]

An international manhunt in the coming months resulted in the capture of white segregationist James Earl Ray, who fled to England after the assassination. Tennessee prosecutors agreed to a plea bargain in which Ray admitted guilt in return for a sentence of life imprisonment rather than the death penalty. Over the years, Ray attempted various legal maneuvers to reverse his conviction—retracting his confession, claiming that he was framed, and insisting that a larger conspiracy lay behind the death of King. By the time of Ray's death in 1998, many members of the King family supported Ray's appeal for a new trial, and King's son, Dexter Scott King, publicly stated his belief that Ray was innocent. As in the case of the assassination of President Kennedy in 1963, conspiracy theories continue to surround the shooting of King.

THE VISION

In 1962 Ralph Allen was a student at Connecticut's Trinity College. Inspired by the civil rights marches, Allen and some of his friends decided to travel to Albany, Georgia to help in the voter registration drive. Working with local civil rights leaders and members of King's organization, they canvassed neighborhoods and organized meetings to help spread the message about voting rights.

During that summer and the next, Allen met King, Andrew Young, Stokely Carmichael, James Farmer and many other prominent civil rights leaders. Allen and his friends avoided most of the sit-ins and mass demonstrations and concentrated on the less confrontational aspects of voter registration. Nevertheless, they were arrested numerous times in general roundups by local police attempting to slow down progress being made in signing up black voters.

At the Mt. Olive Baptist Church in Sasser, the group held weekly meetings on canvassing and other aspects of the voter registration campaign and gathered to pray and sing freedom songs. In mid-July, one of the weekly meetings was suddenly visited by Sheriff Zeke T. Mathews and 15 or 20 deputized white citizens with nightsticks. The sheriff proceeded to go from person to person interrogating them in a mockingly friendly but threatening manner. To the leader of the gathering, Lucius Holloway, the sheriff remarked that none of the blacks in the room that night, including Holloway, had ever wanted to vote until the outside agitators had arrived and stirred things up and "put these dang fool ideas in your head."[5]

In late August, Mt. Olive Church was firebombed to the ground early one Sunday morning. The civil rights leaders called King in Atlanta. Although he was scheduled to preach at Ebenezer that morning, he and some friends drove to Alabama to be with the people who had lost their church.

Ralph Allen remembered the camaraderie and comfort that King engendered, the sense that they were all in this together, like a congregation. They gathered in the open near a cotton field and King preached. "We will rebuild this church," King declared. "They prayed and sang freedom songs," said Allen. "At the end we all gathered in a circle and crossed our arms, each person holding hands with the person on either side and sang 'We Shall Overcome.' In Southwest Georgia the way it ends is everybody hums the song and anybody who's moved to say or pray anything goes ahead and does it. Rev. Wells from Albany, who would later go to work for Dr. King's Southern Christian Leadership Conference, he prayed, and Sherrod prayed. My friend Chris Potter ... describes good friends as those who 'you can call late, and they'll come early.' That's the kind of person Dr. King was. That's the point I want to make about him. In addition to being a visionary, a deeply inspiring writer and speaker, and a man of such courage he could walk daily joking with the shadow of death, he was a 'call late and come early' friend to whole communities of people he didn't even know."[6]

Friend, leader, and, eventually, a symbol, Martin Luther King, Jr. was first and foremost a preacher. His roots, talents, and the way he viewed the world all sprang from the earliest lessons from his family and the African American church ministers that he, often reluctantly, listened to in the pews of Ebenezer and other churches. Although his inclinations in his early years veered away from simple faith and unquestioned scriptural truths, he remained, throughout his life, a preacher, one who saw possibilities in the midst of despair and the chance for justice in a world of injustice.

In his speech at the Lincoln Memorial in 1963, King melded religious belief with a call for national mobilization. In the middle of the speech, he brushed aside his notes, locked his eyes squarely on the thousands gathered around the reflecting pool, and offered his vision. Mostly it was a vision squarely from the gospel, this dream of God's children, black and white, rich and poor, gathered in respect and love. A dream unattainable it might have been, but the message left an impression of mutual kinship both powerful and lasting. All of it, King said—the vision, the gains large and small, the steps toward reconciliation—all of it was worth the commitment to try.

They could never be satisfied, he said, as long as blacks were still denied their rights as God's people. And, using the words of the Prophet Amos as he had done that first night of the Montgomery Bus Boycott, he said that they could never be satisfied until "justice rolls down like waters, and righteousness like a mighty stream."[7]

NOTES

1. "Memphis: We Remember, I've Been to the Mountaintop," www.afscme. org/about/kingspch.htm.

2. "On the Balcony with Dr. King," www.explorefaith.org/reflections52. htm.

3. Michael Honey, "A Dream Deferred," *Nation,* May 3, 2004, p. 36.

4. "Benjamin Mays Delivers King eulogy," http://www.bates.edu/x49908. xml.

5. "Friendship: Ralph Allen Remembers the Reverend Martin Luther King, Jr.," http://www.germantownacademy.org/faculty/think-about-it/Allen.

6. "Friendship: Ralph Allen Remembers."

7. Amos 5:24.

SELECTED BIBLIOGRAPHY

BOOKS

Abernathy, Ralph. *And the Walls Came Tumbling Down*. New York: Harper and Row, 1989.

Branch, Taylor. *Parting the Waters: America in the King Years 1954–63*. New York: Touchstone, 1988.

Caro, Robert A. *Master of the Senate*. New York: Alfred A. Knopf, 2002.

Carson, Clayborne, ed. *The Papers of Martin Luther King, Jr.* Vol. 1. *Called to Serve*. Berkeley: University of California Press, 1992.

———. *Autobiography of Martin Luther King, Jr.* New York: Warner Books, 1998.

Dyson, Michael Eric Dyson. *I May Not Get There with You: The True Martin Luther King, Jr.* New York: Touchstone, 2000.

Frady, Marshall. *Martin Luther King, Jr.* New York: Viking, Penguin, 2002.

Free at Last: A History of the Civil Rights Movement and Those Who Died in the Struggle. Montgomery, Ala.: Southern Poverty Law Center, 2004.

Garrow, David J. *Bearing the Cross*. New York: William Morrow, 1986.

Jordan, Vernon E. *Vernon Can Read: A Memoir*. New York: Basic Books, 2001.

Kasher, Steven. *The Civil Rights Movement: A Photographic History, 1954–68*. New York: Abbeville Press, 1996.

King, Coretta Scott. *My Life with Martin Luther King, Jr.* New York: Holt, Rinehart, and Winston, 1969.

King, Martin Luther, Jr. *Stride Toward Freedom*. New York: Harper and Row, 1958.

King, Martin Luther, Sr., with Clayton Riley, *Daddy King: An Autobiography*. New York: William Morrow, 1980.

Kotz, Nick. *Judgment Days: Lyndon Baines Johnson, Martin Luther King, Jr. and the Laws That Changed America.* Boston: Houghton Mifflin, 2005.

Levy, Peter B.,ed. *Documentary History of the Modern Civil Rights Movement.* Westport, Conn.: Greenwood Press, 1992.

Lewis, David L. *King: A Critical Biography.* Westport, Conn: Praeger, 1970.

McWhorter, Diane. *Carry Me Home.* New York: Simon and Schuster, 2001.

Mighty Times: The Legacy of Rosa Parks. Teaching Tolerance, a Project of the Southern Poverty Law Center: 2002.

Nunnelly, William A. *Bull Connor.* Tuscaloosa: University of Alabama Press, 1991.

Oates, Stephen B. *Let the Trumpet Sound: The Life of Martin Luther King, Jr.* New York: New American Library, 1982.

Rosenberg, Jonathan, and Zachary Karabel. *Kennedy, Johnson, and the Quest for Justice: The Civil Rights Tapes.* New York: W. W. Norton, 2003.

Wilkins, Roger. *A Man's Life: An Autobiography.* New York: Simon and Schuster, 1982.

Williams, Juan. *Eyes on the Prize: America's Civil Rights Years, 1954–1965.* New York: Viking Penguin, 1987.

Young, Andrew. *An Easy Burden: The Civil Rights Movement and the Transformation of America.* New York: HarperCollins, 1996.

PERIODICALS

"Attack on the Conscience." *Time.* February 18, 1957, p. 17.

Barrett, George. "Jim Crow, He's Real Tired." *New York Times Magazine.* March 2, 1957, p. 11.

"Black Pocketbook Power." *Time.* March 1, 1968, p. 17.

Cose, Ellis. "Back on the Bridge." *Newsweek.* August 8, 2005, p. 30.

"Integration: 'Full-Scale Assault.'" *Newsweek.* February 29, 1960, p. 25.

"Man of the Year: Never Again Where He Was." *Time.* January 3, 1964, p. 15.

Ralph, James, Jr. "Dr. King and the Chicago Freedom Movement." *American Visions.* August/September 1994, p. 30.

Rowan, John. "Dr. King's Dinner." *American Heritage.* February 2000, p. 28.

Stone, Chuck. "Selma to Montgomery." *National Geographic.* February 2000, p. 98.

"Up From Jim Crow." *Newsweek.* September 18, 2000, p. 42.

Wainwright, Loudon. "Martyr of the Sit-ins." *Life.* November 7, 1960, p. 123.

Weisenburger, Steven. "Bloody Sunday." *Southwest Review,* 2005, p. 175.

Wilkins, Roger. "Benjamin Mays." *Nation,* July 21, 2003, p. 28.

INTERNET

"American RadioWorks—"The President Calling." http://americanradioworks. publicradio.org/features/prestapes/c1.html.

Bennett, Lerone, Jr. "The Last of the Great Schoolmasters." *Ebony*. September 2004. http://www.findarticles.com/p/articles/mi_m1077/is_11_59/ai_n6172408.

Carson, Clayborne, ed. *The Autobiography of Martin Luther King, Jr.* http://www.stanford.edu/group/King/publications,autobiography/chp_21.htm.

Elliot, Debbie. "Wallace in the Schoolhouse Door." http://www.npr.org/templates/story/story.php?storyId=1294.

"The Ethical Foundations of Dr. King's Political Action, Remarks of Charles V. Willie, Charles William Eliot Professor of Education, Emeritus, on the occasion of Martin Luther King Jr. Day, January 21, 2002, The Memorial Church, Harvard University." http://www.news.harvard.edu/gazette/2002/01.17/99-mlkspeech.html.

"Eulogy for the Young Victims of the Sixteenth Street Baptist Church Bombing, Delivered at Sixth Avenue Baptist Church." http://www.stanford.edu/group/King/speeches/pub/Eulogy_for_the_martyred_children.html.

Formwalt, Lee W. "Moving forward by recalling the past...." http://members.surfsouth.com/~mtzion/movementhistory.htm.

"Freedom Rides." http://www.watson.org/~lisa/blackhistory/civilrights-55–65/freeride.html.

Gittinger, Ted, and Allen Fisher. "LBJ Champions the Civil Rights Act of 1964." http://www.archives.gov/publications/prologue/2004/summer/civil-rights-act-1.html.

"*Martin Luther King: Beyond Vietnam—A Time to Break Silence* delivered 4 April 1967 at a meeting of Clergy and Laity Concerned at Riverside Church in New York City." http://www.americanrhetoric.com/speeches/mlkatimetobreaksilence.htm.

"Martin Luther King's Letter from Birmingham Jail." http://www.citadel-information.com/mlk-letter-from-birmingham-jail.pdf.

"Martin Luther King's Nobel Prize Acceptance Speech." http://www.nobelprizes.com/nobel/peace/MLK-nobel.html.

"M. K. Gandhi Institute for Nonviolence: About Gandhi." http://www.gandhiinstitute.org/AboutGandhi/index.cfm.

President Lyndon B. Johnson's Special Message to the Congress: "The American Promise." March 15, 1965. http://www.lbjlib.utexas.edu/johnson/archives.hom/speeches.hom/650315.asp.

"Press Conference Announcing the Poor People's Campaign." http://www.stanford.edu/group/King/publications/papers/unpub/671204-003_Announcing_Poor_Peoples_campaign.htm.

"Radio and Television Report to the American People on Civil Rights, President John F. Kennedy, June 11, 1963." http://www.jfklibrary.org/j061163.htm.

"*Speeches of Martin Luther King, Jr.*, Statement Delivered at a Rally to Support the Freedom Rides 21 May 1961, Montgomery, Alabama." http://www.

stanford.edu/group/King/publications/speeches/unpub/610521-000_
  Statement_Delivered_at_a_Rally_to_Support_the_Freedom_Rides.html.
Stafford, Tim. "A Fire You Can't Put Out: Remembering Martin Luther King, Jr."
  http://www.christianitytoday.com/books/web/2001/jan17a.html.
"Stokely Carmichael—Black Power." http://www.americanrhetoric.com/speeches/
  stokelycarmichaelblackpower.html.
"Supplementary Detailed Staff Reports on Intelligence Activities and the
  Rights of Americans. Book III, Final Report of the Select Committee to
  Study Governmental Operations with Respect to Intelligence Activities.
  Dr. Martin Luther King, Jr. Case Study." http://www.icdc.com/~paulwolf/
  cointelpro/churchfinalreportIIIb.htm.
"Sweet Chariot: The Story of the Spirituals—Freedom Songs of the Civil
  Rights Movement: Slave Spirituals Revived." http://cctl.du.edu/spirituals/
  freedom/civil.cfm.

MANUSCRIPT COLLECTIONS

The largest collections of papers of Martin Luther King, Jr. are in the Special
  Collections Department of Boston University and in the Martin Luther
  King, Jr. Library and Archives in Atlanta, Georgia.

INDEX

About the Author

ROGER BRUNS is an independent scholar and prolific author of biographies of Billy Graham (Greenwood, 2004), Jesse Jackson (Greenwood, 2005), and many other major figures.